Complete Woodfinishing

REVISED EDITION

Ian Hosker

GUILD OF MASTER CRAFTSMAN PUBLICATIONS LTD

First published 2003 by
Guild of Master Craftsman Publications Ltd
166 High Street, Lewes
East Sussex BN7 1XU

Reprinted 2003, 2005

ISBN 1 86108 247 9

British Cataloguing in Publication Data
A catalogue record of this book is available from the British Library.

Production Manager: Hilary MacCallum
Managing Editor: Gerrie Purcell
Editor: Gill Parris
Design: Ian Hunt Design
Illustrations: @ Tim Benké 2003

Typeface: Scala Regular and Scala Sans

Colour separation by Articolour Italia Srl (Italy)

Printed and bound by Kyodo (Singapore)

PHOTOGRAPHIC CREDITS

Anthony Bailey, GMC Publications Photographic Studio: cover, pp. 2, 8, 10 (x 2), 11 (x 2), 12 (x 3), 15, 23 (top), 24, 26, 29, 34, 46, 48–50, 52, 54 (x 2), 55 (x 2), 56 (x 4), 57 (x 2), 61–2 (x 2), 65 (x 4), 68, 70, 74 (x 2), 75, 82, 90, 94, 100, 104, 110, 117, 121–3,129 (x 3), 134, 154, 158 and 162.
Ian Hosker: pp. 4, 5 (x 2), 30–2, 39; 41 (x 2), 43, 51, 69, 98, 101 (x 2), 102 (x 2), 103, 107, 111, 118, 126, 130, 136–8, 141, 143, 144 (x 2), 145–6, 147 (x 3), 148 (x 2), 149 (x 2), 151 (x 4), 153 (x 4), 156–7, 159 (x 2) and 160.
Mark Baker: 16, 106 (x 2), 108 (x 2) and 109 (x 3).
John Lloyd: p. 14.
Keith Welters: 44.

Other photographs supplied courtesy of the following manufacturers:

GT French Polishing: 124.
ITW Industrial Finishing: 22, 23 (bottom), 85, 86 (x 2), 87 (x 2) and 91.
Rentokil Property Care: 113 (x 2), 114 (x 2), 115 (x 2) and 120 (x 2).
Screwfix Direct: 88 and 89.

ACKNOWLEDGEMENT

The Publishers would like to thank Anthony Bailey for help above and beyond the call of duty.

Complete
Woodfinishing

REVISED EDITION

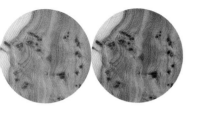

Contents

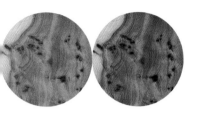 # Introduction

There have been advances in the technology of woodfinishing since the first edition of this book was published and in this revised edition I have updated all chapters to take account of these. For example, Chapter 14 on Special Paint Effects has been rewritten because of the introduction of entirely new products in the marketplace, which make this field of wood decoration more accessible to a wider audience. All other chapters have modifications based on continuing experience, feedback from readers and students, new materials and methods and the changes in my teaching methods that I have adopted since writing the first edition.

My aim is to help you to enjoy the craft of woodfinishing by describing techniques that are known to work, and showing you how to develop levels of skill that will satisfy you and others who matter to you. There is nothing in this book that cannot be achieved through the acquisition of knowledge and experience, although some techniques may be impractical because of limitations of workshop space and facilities. And on this last point, I emphasize the importance of safe working practices, so this may be a restricting factor that prevents you from adopting spraying techniques, for instance.

The Internet has made it an easy task to find accurate information about suppliers of materials, both at the local and national level, so I haven't included a list of suppliers in this book. In the UK, for example, you can search Yellow Pages online (www.yell.com) and obtain up-to-date contact details for any supplier listed. Search engines are also powerful tools for tracking down suppliers, and they have become more reliable and easier to use in recent years. Many suppliers' sites also provide comprehensive product listings and technical data.

Even given these advances in woodfinishing and information technology, the craft of woodfinishing is one to be enjoyed, and the purpose of this new edition remains the same as that of the first: learn, practise, master, but also enjoy working with colour, texture and light. Always regard your own woodfinishing as a learning activity – and an enormously satisfying one at that. There is nothing quite like the buzz generated by seeing the product of your own practical endeavours.

You have my very best wishes.

Ian Hosker

1 The Right Finish for the Job

Having finally completed that table you have been mulling over for the last few months, how are you going to finish it? If you were planning to apply a couple of coats of polyurethane, and hope that it would pass muster, you should give it more serious thought.

Although there is absolutely nothing wrong with polyurethane, as you will discover later in this book, perhaps there is something better. Before finding out what, if anything, is better, consider why we bother with a finish in the first place. Essentially, we are putting on some form of colouring and/or coating material:

- To enhance the natural beauty of wood's grain texture and surface markings (referred to as 'figure').
- To produce an even colour and surface that is pleasing to look at and which fits in well with its surroundings.
- To protect the wood from a wide variety of things that will destroy, damage or disfigure it in some way.

It is a well-worn cliché, used in all books on woodfinishing, that many a good piece of craftsmanship is ruined by poor finishing. For generations the crafts of the cabinetmaker and the polisher have been separate, and perhaps that should tell us something. However, there is no real excuse for bodging. Not everyone is comfortable with, or highly skilled in applying, French polish, but there are alternatives that can make the work look just as good. So, why is there this problem?

- Lack of knowledge, skill and experience of the wide range of finishing materials that are now available to both professionals and amateurs.

- Lack of planning. Finishing is often left out of the 'thinking it through' process and, consequently, very little attention is given to it.

Planning is a matter of good working practice. Before you touch the first piece of wood to start your project, you should already know what its final surface will look like, because you will have asked yourself a number of questions which will set the criteria for choosing a finish. The questions you should ask are:

- Will it have to be a particular colour?
- Will it be handled a great deal?
- Will it be subjected to possible water or alcohol spillages?
- Will it be subjected to having hot objects placed upon it?
- Will it look better as a high gloss, low lustre or totally matt?
- Is the object under consideration going to be indoors or out?
- What skills do I possess?
- Is the nature of the wood itself going to determine the best method of finishing (i.e. is there an attractive figure that needs to be brought out, or is the wood likely to reject certain finishes)?
- Is there a traditional way of finishing this particular wood and do I want to reproduce that traditional look on this piece?
- Does the piece have to match other items?

Not all of these questions need to be asked every time, and there may even be others that occur to you at the time, but the need to include some thought on finishing at the planning stage of your project cannot be overstressed, as it may sometimes influence other factors. For example, it is sometimes better to stain and polish components that are difficult to reach before assembly and so, without forward planning, you could make life difficult for yourself.

THE WRONG FINISH

It is not just a question of making life a little bit easier. There can be unfortunate and disappointing consequences if the wrong type of finish is applied, if the type of stain is incompatible with the polish material or solvent, or if incorrect surface preparation has taken place.

Fig 1.1 shows an exterior door where the varnish is peeling off and there is bad staining due to moisture. Normal internal polyurethane varnish is unsuitable, as the constant movement of the door, expanding and contracting as atmospheric conditions change, causes it to crack through not being very flexible. This allows water to penetrate and lift the varnish.

Alternatively, it could be that moisture was trapped in the wood prior to finishing, or the stain used was not quite dry. The result would be the same. One of the humidity resistant varnishes would have been better (see Chapter 8). They are able to tolerate slightly higher levels of moisture in the wood, allowing water vapour to escape through the varnish film. These exterior-quality varnishes are also better able to tolerate the natural expansion and shrinkage of timber that is exposed to wide fluctuations in climatic conditions.

Fig 1.2 shows the badly ring-marked and scratched surface of a French-polished table. This very beautiful but vulnerable finish is not resistant to heat, alcohol or moisture. Perhaps, in this case, an acid-cured lacquer (see Chapter 9), or even a burnished polyurethane varnish (see Chapter 8) might have been better. Both categories of materials are more tolerant to heat and spillages.

On page 6 there is a flowchart to help you decide upon the best finish for the job in hand. By answering the questions, you will be led step by step to those that seem to fit the bill. You will also be directed to the appropriate sections of the book where you can read up on your chosen finish.

Fig 1.1 Exterior-grade varnish, while tough, will eventually break down under the constant onslaught of weather, existing dampness in the wood and physical use.

Fig 1.2 French polish is vulnerable to moisture, heat, alcohol and other solvents. Here, a white ring mark has been caused by a wet glass or cup being left on the surface for some time.

Chapters 4 and 5 are obligatory reading, as the procedures are the same, no matter what you plan to do, as they contain information about certain stains that are potentially incompatible with the final polish, which should be checked before continuing.

TRADITIONAL FINISHING OF SOME TIMBERS

Just because something is traditionally done it does not, of course, bind you to doing the same, but it might influence your final choice, as traditions are based on what experience shows to work. Oak, pine and teak seem to please the eye more when they are finished to a low lustre (see Fig 1.3). Oak has a rustic image; its coarse-grain texture and medullary-ray figuring on quarter-sawn boards are certainly shown off at their best if the grain is left open (i.e. no grain filler has been used) and there is high build-up of polish. This creates the impression that you are touching the wood itself when you run your fingers over it, which many people would be tempted to do.

Pine is a curious one, in that it is widely regarded as a 'show' timber. In fact, pine furniture historically was quite ordinary and cheap, and often relegated to the servants' working and living areas, or other low-status domestic areas. Pine was also used as a base for high-quality painted furniture. A number of coats of gesso (see Chapter 14) were applied, and were then sanded to mirror-smoothness before applying decorative paint.

Fig 1.3 The low lustre of pine suits its 'rustic' and functional appearance. Waxing or even oiling will achieve this effect. The finish on this door is matt polyurethane varnish because it is subject to much wear and tear. The overall effect is the same.

Walnut, mahogany and rosewood look superb under carefully applied French polish, where the optical qualities seem to enhance the attractive and dramatic figures characteristic of these timbers. They look equally good under modern synthetic spray lacquers, carefully applied and hand finished (see Chapter 9).

Oak was traditionally waxed, oiled or simply burnished, its rustic surface-texture and figure being allowed to speak for itself.

In the end, however, it is your decision as to how you finish your project; it only matters that, at the end of the day, it is pleasing to look at and is durable enough for its purpose. The point is you must take account of purpose, decorative requirements and anticipated wear. Cost, in terms of materials and labour, is a legitimate factor, but should be secondary to durability, function and decorative effect.

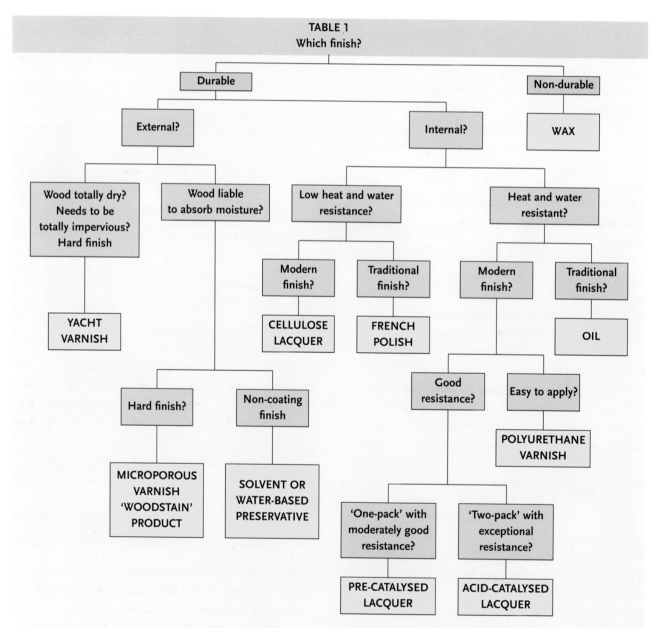

TABLE 1
Which finish?

CHOOSING A FINISH

The Table on the facing page can be used to guide you towards an appropriate finish for the job in hand, but there may be other overriding factors to take into account.

Starting at the top, follow the arrows that give the appropriate criteria. For example, if the surface needs to be durable, you are led to the questions 'internal?' or 'external?' Assuming the work is external, is it liable to be absorbing a lot of moisture, or do you suspect that moisture may be there already? If the answer is yes, do you want a hard finish or a finish that is non-coating? Hard finish leads you to use microporous materials, and non-coating leads to solvent- or oil-based preservative.

As I say, this is only a guide, and you may find that when you turn to the appropriate chapters the finish may not be exactly what you are looking for. An alternative should then be sought, but this may mean compromising on specifications. For example, you may decide on French polish, and therefore compromise on heat and water resistance.

MATERIALS AND METHODS

The great thing about finishing as a craft is that the tools and materials required to perform the task are relatively few, compared to other crafts associated with woodworking. Nevertheless, a rough understanding of what the tools and material are, and how they are used, is vital if you are to achieve a decent finish. Where appropriate, an explanation of methods and materials has been provided.

Finally, at the end of the book, Chapter 16 is devoted to recipes for making polishes, cleaners, revivers, and a number of other useful substances the polisher may need and which can be successfully home-made in small or large batches.

METHOD OF WORKING

I have already mentioned that many problems and disappointments arise through poor planning, or even no real planning at all. You must know in advance what procedures are needed. You need to be meticulous in your approach to the work and, above all, do not rush things. If a varnish requires six hours to dry sufficiently before applying another coat, then leave it for six hours. This may sound patronizing, but sometimes the temptation to rush things can be overwhelming. On occasion I have been so pushed for time that I have had to walk away from the job for the day and put it out of my mind to reduce the frustration.

In general, the order of working is as follows:

- Prepare the surface by filling or repairing blemishes, and smoothing

- Stain (if required)

- Fill the grain (if required)

- Apply an initial coat of polish

- Correct any colour errors (if appropriate)

- Apply finishing coats of polish

It is usual (except in the case of waxing and oiling) to gently rub down the surface between coats, partly to remove adhering particles but also to provide a key for the subsequent coat.

COMPATIBILITY

One of the most frequent questions asked is 'what can be used on what?'. Compatibility is an important issue in woodfinishing, especially now the range of products and their formulations is so large and diverse. Mistakes can be expensive, so I will address the issue of compatibility throughout the book. The last thing you want is for a perfect finish to be spoiled because it starts to flake off several weeks later.

Perhaps one of the best pieces of advice I can give is to find a range of products from one or two manufacturers that you feel comfortable with. Manufacturers tend to produce ranges that include matched products, e.g. wood dyes, sealers, finishing coats and grain fillers. Get to know them and their characteristics, especially how they work together.

2 Power Sanding

No book on woodfinishing can be complete without a detailed explanation of how to achieve a surface suitable for taking a fine finish. A great deal will be made of meticulous surface preparation from Chapter 4 onwards, but there is a stage prior to this where some heavy work may be required to remove uneven surfaces and blemishes before the final hand preparation of the surface.

There is a place for powered sanding tools, as they make this work quicker and less laborious, but the surface produced by a machine is rarely good enough to take any of the fine finishes, such as French polish. Wax and oil finishes are less demanding on surface quality but, even so, care needs to be taken to prevent the sanding process creating its own imperfections in the surface.

There are two main types of sanding machines used for initial preparation of the surface: belt and orbital. Because the process of sanding is based on scratching away the surface with an abrasive material, it is fairly obvious that the abrasive will leave its own marks. It is important that the abrasion takes place along the grain, otherwise there will be marks that show through the final finish, no matter how careful you have been. (See Chapter 4 for more details.)

Power sanding machines should be kept on the move all the time and should not be allowed to dwell on a single spot for any length of time, as this would create hollows, or cut through veneers. It is important to stop the machine as dust begins to build up on the surface, and clear it away, as this dust is a mixture of wood and abrasive particles, which will scratch the surface if allowed to accumulate between the machine and the wood surface. Always use a machine with a dust extraction connector that can be used either with an industrial dust extraction unit, or a workshop vacuum cleaner.

BELT SANDER

As its name implies, a belt of abrasive runs over two rollers, with the working face running over a smooth metal base-plate which presses the belt onto the substrate. Industrial sanding machines can be quite huge (see Figs 2.1a and 2.1b overleaf). The abrasive power of belt sanders is such that the belt needs to be constructed of very tough abrasives and the backing material of stiff woven fabric. This combination makes them both durable and expensive consumables.

Hand-held sanders are very useful for the initial preparation prior to hand sanding or using an orbital sander. They are designed to move material rapidly, and are frequently used to prepare the surface after it has been planed (see Figs 2.2a and b on page 11).

As will be seen in Chapter 4, machine planing does not produce a satisfactory surface, and belt sanding is often a really good way of quickly smoothing out the blemishes. A good craftsman with a well-honed and finely adjusted smoothing plane can produce an almost perfect surface by hand. Belt sanders are not suitable for use on a veneered surface because of the rapid removal of wood.

As you push the machine along the wood (using only the weight of the machine itself, with virtually no downward pressure), the area of the belt in contact with the substrate opposes the movement of the tool. This

Fig 2.1 (a) An industrial belt sander designed for large production work.

Fig 2.1 (b) Belt sander/linisher designed for small workshop use.

Fig 2.2 (a) Hand-held belt sander with sanding frame for controlling depth of cut and adding stability.

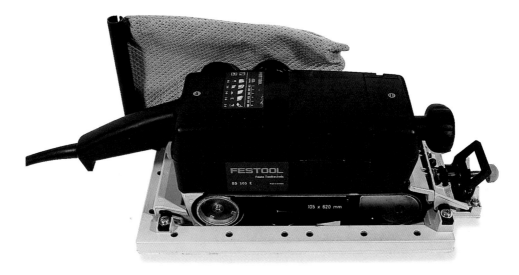

Fig 2.2 (b) When the sanding frame is removed, the machine can get into smaller spaces and butt up against internal sides.

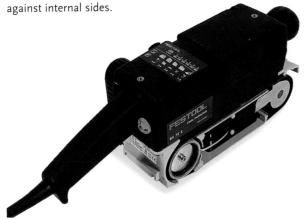

gives two advantages: friction, so that the cutting action is increased, and better control.

The belt sander is also invaluable for cleaning off wide, flat surfaces made up of butt-jointed boards. Uneven joints can be levelled and exuded glue removed, but note that glue quickly clogs the abrasive.

Though it might seem a contradiction of what was said earlier about not using abrasive material across the grain, the belt sander does work better if it is allowed to cut at a very slight angle to the grain direction (see Fig 2.3), thus producing a guillotine action.

Final sanding is then achieved either by hand, or with an orbital sander.

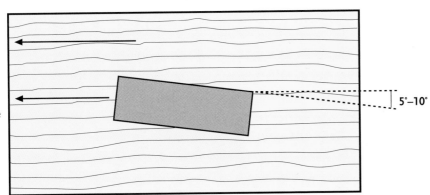

General line of direction

Direction of sander across the work

5°–10°

Fig 2.3 A hand-held belt sander should be presented at a slight angle to the general grain direction to improve its cutting power.

Belt sander presented at slight angle to grain direction

ORBITAL SANDER

This is a final smoothing tool, rather than a machine designed to remove a large amount of material (see Fig 2.4). Consequently, it should always be used with fine grades of abrasive paper.

The machine works by rotating its base around a fixed position (hence the term orbital), so that each grain of abrasive actually rotates in a circle over the surface, effectively scouring the surface. This is done at very high speed, and the diameter of rotation is very small indeed (see Fig 2.5). Problems arise if you use an orbital sander with coarse paper grades, as the grains of abrasive leave behind a very large number of tiny circular scratches which are very difficult to remove later without resorting to a belt sander.

Fig 2.4 An orbital sander

Fig 2.6 (a) A palm sander.

Individual grain of abrasive when pad is static

Base of sander

Rotary path taken by grain of abrasive when sander is switched on

Fig 2.5 Orbital sanding works by rotating the abrasive material in a circular path of very small radius at very high speed, effectively scouring the surface.

Fig 2.6 (b) Detail sanders are a variant of the palm sander.

Another point to bear in mind is that it is inadvisable to use excessive pressure, as this will only lead to a poor-quality surface being produced and overloading of the motor, reducing the life of the machine. As with the hand-held belt sander, use only the pressure caused by the weight of the machine.

The action of an orbital sander is very gentle and can be used with reasonable confidence on veneered work, providing very fine grades of abrasive paper are used (see Chapter 4). However, still take care when refinishing pieces, as the veneer is probably very thin.

Orbital sanders can be moved over the whole surface in any direction. The rotation of the base makes the rule of moving only along the grain pretty pointless.

Palm sanders are small orbital sanders that fit snugly into the palm of one hand, which makes them useful for small and awkward areas such as the insides of drawers (see Fig 2.6a). A 'detail sander' (Fig 2.6b) is a variant of the palm sander. Its triangular sole creates a point that can get into tight and awkward corners.

USEFUL FEATURES OF POWER SANDERS

As a general rule, you should always buy the tools and equipment that you can afford but, if you intend to do a lot of work, it does pay to invest in quality. 'Horses for courses' applies here, as the quality of powered equipment varies markedly and the market consists of different levels: need, and depth of pockets. Not long ago, tools were relatively so expensive that it was tempting to invest in attachments for the humble power drill. This is not the case now, as the price of these tools has plummeted in real terms and the quality of the machines has also increased; this is mainly due to improvements in technology, manufacturing techniques and materials, so they tend to be lighter in weight, better powered and less tiring to use.

HAND-HELD BELT SANDER

The features to look for are the width of the belt, the speed, and the power of the motor. Widths range from 2in (51mm) on DIY models to about 4in (102mm) on professional hand-held machines. The average length of the sanding area is about 6in (152mm). The width and speed also determine the power of the motor needed to drive it. Obviously, the wider the belt, the greater the area in contact with the substrate, and the greater the frictional force. A more powerful motor will be needed to overcome this force and drive the belt around without strain and at a good speed. The problem then becomes that of weight. A good compromise is a machine with a 3in (76mm) belt. Belt speeds vary from about 300–500m (325–550yds) per minute.

The depth of cut can be controlled with a sanding frame fixed to the base of the sander, which may be adjusted to vary the cut. This also increases the area of the base overall, so helps to keep a flat surface.

Another useful controlling device is variable speed: for a relatively modest additional cost, machines with electronic speed control can increase the versatility of the machine. However, this facility is not essential in a belt sander.

ORBITAL SANDERS

The faster the speed of the orbital action, the finer the finish that will be achieved. Again, electronic speed controls are available on some models, though this is not essential. The average orbital speed is in the order of 4000–5000 orbits per minute, but the more expensive machines can take this up into five figures.

These sanders are the genuine article when determining what is a finishing power tool. If very fine grades of abrasive are used, e.g. 240 grit (see Chapter 4), exceptionally fine surfaces can be obtained on suitable substrates. In fact, this machine can be used to de-nib between coats of varnish or lacquer (but not French polish). The palm sander is particularly effective for this.

Orbital sanders are sized according to the area of the sanding base. They come in three basic sizes: third sheet, half sheet and quarter sheet. These sizes refer to the proportion of a standard sheet of abrasive paper 11 x 9in (279 x 229mm) to be fitted. A half sheet machine is the best choice for most purposes, while the quarter sheet models are the palm sanders.

SAFETY

A sanding machine should be switched on before being presented to the surface. Starting it up while it is in contact will create a dangerous torque that can wrench the machine from your grip and conceivably cause injury. It should also be lifted from the surface before being switched off. Most machines have a button which, when depressed, keeps the motor running without using the trigger switch. This does have obvious advantages in that it prevents hand fatigue during periods of extended operation but, while I am an enthusiastic user of this button, there is one reservation which you should be aware of: what happens if, for some reason, you lose your grip on the machine? The sight of a machine pirouetting away beyond your reach,

to wreak damage elsewhere, is not one to be repeated. The trigger switch doubles up as a 'dead man's switch' – let go, and the machine's motor stops.

The way these machines are held during operation is particularly important. You must keep control at all times. Fig 2.7 shows how both hands are used to maintain the sanding area in contact with the surface. Particular care needs to be taken when the machine reaches the ends and edges, to prevent it from dropping over. Fig 2.8, on the facing page, shows how the pressure applied by the hands, light though it is, becomes transferred from one hand to the other as the sander reaches the ends. The positioning of the hands in Fig 2.7 is the same for orbital sanders (except palm sanders, of course, which are operated with one hand only).

Fig 2.7 Belt and orbital sanders should be held securely with both hands.

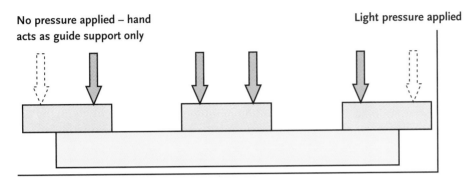

No pressure applied – hand acts as guide support only

Light pressure applied

Fig 2.8 Transfer hand pressure from one hand to another as the sander approaches the ends of the work.

Fig 2.8 (a) The overlapping portion of the sanding area does not drop over the edge, causing rounding over. This is particularly important on veneered work, where the edges are vulnerable to being worn through.

Fig 2.8 (b) Light pressure maintained to ensure uniform contact with the wood along the entire length and width of the sanding area.

There are two other areas of concern when using machinery of this type: electrical safety, dust and noise. Electrical safety is much less of a concern than it once was, as safety standards dictate that machines are 'double insulated' and that the power and the operator are kept well apart. The cases of hand power tools are now plastic, which affords additional protection. Even so, common sense dictates that they must not be used where water is likely to come into contact with them. In addition, an operator can become so immersed in the job that it is quite easy to snag the cable with the abrasive, and so a circuit breaker also makes sense.

What causes great concern, though, is pollution, both noise and dust. The effect of noise cannot be ignored, as it is cumulative and generally irreversible. Many occasions of extended periods of machine noise can damage your hearing, and so the use of ear defenders is a must (see Fig 2.9). If you haven't used them before, you will be surprised by the amount of sound that can get through: they reduce the level of machine noise without deafening you to other sounds, and you can hold a perfectly intelligible conversation while wearing ear defenders.

The effect of dust is also cumulative in its damaging effect on the lungs. Always wear a mask and eye shields, in case anything is thrown up by the machine, and use a dust extraction system. See Chapter 3 for a more detailed explanation of health and safety issues.

Fig 2.9 Ear defenders reduce the volume of sound reaching the operator's ears and remove or reduce the frequencies that cause permanent hearing damage.

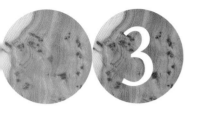

3 Health and Safety

The romantic figure of the French polisher huddled over some gleaming piece of furniture, lovingly caressing it with gently curving sweeps of a polish-filled pad, still figures very strongly in the minds of many people. This ideal evokes images of contentment, harmony and pride in craftsmanship, and those people of an age where they can remember people working in this way may even recall the atmosphere and smells in those workshops.

While the traditional French polisher is still alive and kicking, the nature of woodfinishing has changed beyond all recognition. No longer are we dealing simply with beeswax and turpentine, linseed oil, alcohol and shellac in French polish, and other such goodies. There are now some very nasty substances that have been developed to answer the call for cost-efficient coatings with improved mechanical properties. The irony is that while we apply these substances to protect the surface of wood, the woodfinisher frequently needs to be protected against their potentially harmful effects.

It is the mark of a civilized society that we believe in protecting citizens from the harmful activities of other people, or from the dangers posed by the results of those activities. As far as the woodfinisher is concerned, the two most important pieces of legislation that affect his or her working life are the Health and Safety at Work Act 1974, and the Control of Substances Hazardous to Health (COSHH) Regulations 1999. To these two cornerstones must be added specific legislation governing the use of particular materials. Taking a wider view, environmental legislation has been designed to prevent pollution and, consequently, prevent harm to animals, plants and humans.

HEALTH AND SAFETY AT WORK ACT 1974, AND COSHH

It is not my intention to discuss these laws and regulations in detail, as this is not really within the scope of woodfinishing. However, they are of such importance that any book on the subject must raise awareness of their existence and importance. Anyone wishing to pursue more detailed knowledge should contact their local Environmental Health Department or regional office of the Health and Safety Executive (HSE). There is also a wealth of free and priced information available from the HSE which contains the current position with regard to regulations, state of knowledge about hazards and risks, and guidance information. Some of this can be obtained directly from the HSE website (www.hse.gov.uk). Refer to these sources for up to date information and guidance.

The Health and Safety at Work Act is a piece of umbrella legislation, not only providing protection under the terms as originally drawn up in the early 1970s, but also empowering the Health and Safety Executive, through the government of the day, to introduce regulations that strengthen the law. One of the most important of these sets of regulations is the Control of Substances Hazardous to Health Regulations (COSHH). These regulations first came into effect in October 1989, and are a very powerful addition to the law. They have subsequently been revised (1999).

One of the main strengths of the COSHH regulations is the way in which they have involved everyone in the process of identifying potentially harmful substances in their working environment and in producing strategies to minimize risk, as well as continuously monitoring the use of hazardous materials. Under the terms of COSHH, all substances that have any potential to harm (as far as such knowledge is available) have to be identified and recorded. For each of these substances a code of practice has to be drawn up, to protect people from levels of exposure considered harmful.

Every year, the HSE publishes a list of known and commonly used hazardous substances and assigns exposure limits to each. This is based on the current state of scientific knowledge, which is why the data is updated annually. The values attached to these limits are referred to as Occupational Exposure Limits (OEL). Each identified hazardous substance has its own OEL (expressed as parts per million or milligrams per cubic metre), and this can be found in the Health and Safety Executive Guidance Notes EH40 Occupational Exposure Limits.

There are two types of OEL: occupational exposure standards (OES) and maximum exposure limits (MELs):

- **OCCUPATIONAL EXPOSURE STANDARDS (OES)** This value is set at a level that is not likely to harm the health of workers exposed to the substance by inhalation day after day. Exposure to the hazardous substance should be controlled to ensure that it complies with its OES. Under COSHH, the OES can be temporarily exceeded so long as the reason for going above the limit is known, and steps are taken to reduce exposure as soon as is reasonably practicable.

- **MAXIMUM EXPOSURE LIMIT (MEL)** This limit is set for substances that may cause serious health effects, such as asthma or cancer, if inhaled. For these substances there are no OES set, and exposure must be reduced to below the MEL.

Inhalation is not the only way that substances can cause harm. Contact with, or absorption through, the skin can also result in harm. In such cases, it will be necessary to protect the body against direct exposure, with the use of personal protective equipment (PPE). The HSE provides guidance on the hazards posed by commonly used products in most industries, and you should refer to this up-to-date information.

The answer, of course, is to remove the hazard (see the section on Risk Assessment). A considerable amount of money is spent by companies on research and development to create products that are based on less harmful materials, and yet retain similar characteristics – and better ones, if possible – to those they are replacing. For example, water-based varnishes have many of the useful properties of oil- and solvent-based products. They are also faster drying, which allows three coats to be applied in one day, and the equipment can be cleaned in water.

CLASSIFICATION, PACKAGING AND LABELLING OF DANGEROUS SUBSTANCES REGULATIONS (1984)

Fig 3.1, on the facing page, shows an example of a container label providing information aimed at warning the user of the hazards associated with the product. This is a legal requirement on all containers holding hazardous materials sold to the public, whether professional users or not. The format of a label as laid down by the CPL Regulations is described below. It is obviously important that the user of any given product is made aware of hazardous substances it contains, so that appropriate risk assessments can be made and control measures implemented.

PRODUCT AND REFERENCE NUMBER
These are specific to the company supplying the product, and are a quick and obvious means of identification.

HAZARDOUS SUBSTANCES
The label must name the substances that pose a hazard.

SUBSTANCE IDENTIFICATION NO. (UN NUMBER)
This is a number that is unique to the hazardous substance and acts as another means of identifying it.

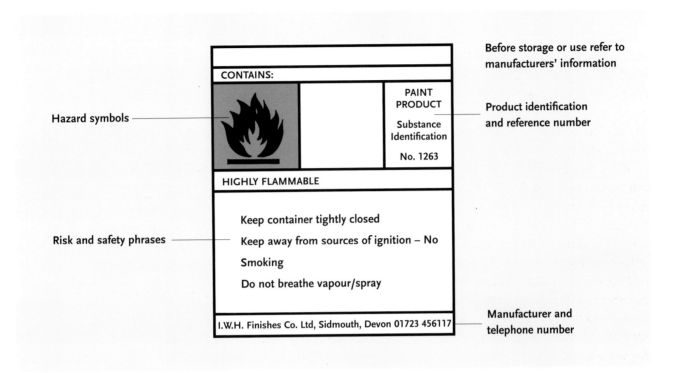

Fig 3.1 Container labelling conforming to the Classification, Packaging and Labelling of Dangerous Substances Regulations 1984.

RISK AND SAFETY PHRASES

These are used to indicate the risks to health that exposure to the substance presents (risk phrases), and to advise on how these risks can be avoided (safety phrases). Up to four risk and four safety phrases may be used. Any more would reduce the impact of the information, because the label is intended to give quick identification of the product and its associated risks.

MANUFACTURER/SUPPLIER

Should the need arise, this information is present so that the company can be contacted regarding any difficulties and at the same time be held accountable.

HAZARD SYMBOLS

There are six basic symbols used to indicate the general nature of the hazard. This immediate recognition of hazard is a ready means of enabling handlers of the product to adopt appropriate procedures. Symbols are also quicker to recognize than lines of text. Fig 3.2, overleaf, shows the internationally recognized hazard symbols that by law must be used on packaging containing a hazardous substance:

- **TOXIC:** Where serious, acute and chronic health risks, and possibly death, may be involved.

- **HARMFUL:** Where limited health risks may be involved.

- **CORROSIVE:** Where contact with living tissues may destroy them.

- **IRRITANT:** Where inflammation may be caused following contact with skin or mucous membranes.

- **HIGHLY FLAMMABLE:** Where the product has a flash point below 22°C (72°F).

- **OXIDIZING:** Where oxygen is released during a chemical reaction.

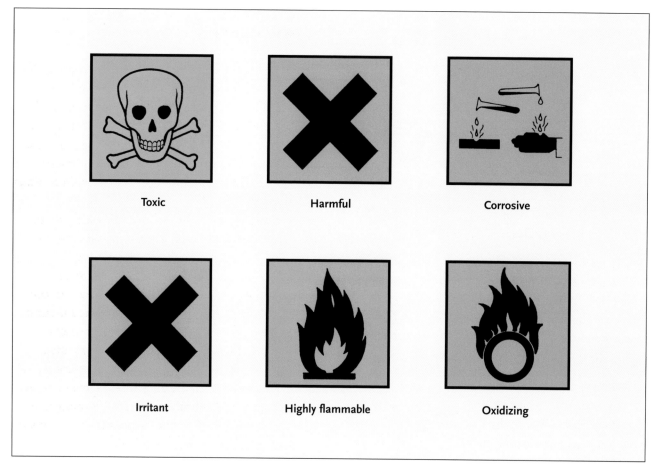

Fig 3.2 The internationally recognized hazard symbols.

These symbols can be used in combination with each other when more than one hazard is involved, i.e. hydrogen peroxide is used as a wood bleach and reacts with any alkaline substance to release chemically active oxygen. This may make it a slight fire risk (although it is not flammable in its own right) but, more importantly, it is corrosive if it comes into contact with your skin. The oxidizing and corrosive symbols would therefore be found together on the packaging.

Manufacturers have to provide comprehensive Health and Safety Data notes for each hazardous product they supply. Apart from a comprehensive description of the hazardous nature of the product, the notes will also include such information as to what precautions should be taken during use; what first aid should be administered in the case of an operator suffering from the effects of exposure; fire prevention; and disposal of the product if it is no longer needed or goes beyond its usable lifespan. Ask for the notes, which will be supplied free.

RISK ASSESSMENT

Whether you are an amateur, or a professional, the importance of undertaking a risk assessment on the materials used cannot be overstressed. Risk assessment applies not only to the materials you use, but also the environment in which you work. The purpose of risk assessment is to remove (not reduce) the risk of harm. The Health and Safety Executive describe a five-step process of risk assessment. There are two key words used in risk assessment: hazard and risk. A hazard is simply anything (product or environmental condition) that can cause harm. A risk is the probability of harm that can be caused by the hazard.

- **STEP 1:** Identify the hazards. The labelling of products or the Health and Safety Data supplied with them will provide much of this information for products. Common sense will often be the best way of identifying environmental hazards such as a blocked doorway, poor lighting or trailing power cables.

- **STEP 2:** Identify the risk (i.e. what harm can be caused) and who is at risk. If you work alone, you are obviously at risk, but there may be others such as your family and neighbours. If you employ staff, they may be at risk, or perhaps your customers may be at risk if they have access to your premises.

- **STEP 3:** Evaluate the risk and determine how risk can be eliminated or controlled. For each of the hazards identified, is the risk high or low? Identify if the risk needs to be controlled by any legal requirement (such as OEL or fire regulations). High-risk hazards need to be dealt with as a matter of urgency.

- **STEP 4:** If you employ staff, the hazards and control measures should be recorded in such a way that they all have access to the information, and are trained to use this information and be aware of risk control. Even if you work alone, recording your findings is not such a bad idea, particularly if this is done in the form of an 'action list' that prioritizes the control measures you intend to introduce.

- **STEP 5:** While primarily aimed at business, this final step is also generally good practice. It is the process of review. Periodically review your risk assessment and revise control measures. Even if you work alone, you may introduce new machinery or use new products or techniques that need to be assessed.

PERSONAL PROTECTIVE EQUIPMENT (PPE): A CASE STUDY

As indicated earlier, risk assessment should, in an ideal world, lead to the removal of risk. For example, if a product is a 'high risk' because of its high volatile solvent content, the ideal control measure is to replace it with a product that has no (or, more realistically, low) risk attached to it. It is this approach to risk assessment that has led to entirely new formulations based on water as the solvent.

However, we do not live in an ideal world, and so compromise is sometimes necessary if a product or process has to be used. The compromise is quite a simple one: if you cannot remove the hazard, and so eliminate the risk, create a protective barrier between the hazard and the person. Under these circumstances, the last resort is to personal protective equipment (PPE). If the risk of harm is high due to inhalation, ingestion or contact (which may include absorption through the skin), then the body must be protected. At various points in this book, you will be recommended to wear gloves, eye-protectors, masks and so on. This is based on the principle just described.

DUST AND VAPOUR
Fig 3.3 (overleaf) is not someone kitted up to enter a nuclear pile, but to spray a noxious lacquer! A finely atomized mist is caused by oversprayed lacquer, paint, etc., and this hangs in the air for a considerable period. The vapour and particulate matter are particular hazards, and there is the risk of fire and explosion.

The overalls are lightweight and made of paper, and are disposable after one wearing. Gloves protect the hands. The headgear is fed with a continuous supply of clean, filtered air which enters over the top of the head and gently downwards over the face, ensuring that any air that may try to enter from the outside is kept out by the tidal stream of fresh air.

This particular system is the top end of the range, and the air fed into the headgear comes from the same airline that feeds the spray equipment, although its pressure is very much reduced. The source of this air is obviously from outside the contaminated area. Cheaper head units can be bought, where the air source is the contaminated area and it is filtered before being pumped across the face. These units are battery operated and, being self-contained, give a considerable degree of freedom to move about.

It follows from the above that, if solvent rapidly evaporates from the oversprayed material, the air will have a high concentration of solvent vapour in it. The equipment shown in Fig 3.3 will provide total protection from exposure. The self-contained, battery operated mask will need to be fitted with a filter that will absorb the vapour. The literature provided with the mask will give information about the types of filter required.

If you are a lone craftsman working on a very tight budget, you may not be willing or able to invest in this expensive equipment. It is possible to buy eye-protectors and respirator masks that still conform to British Standards specifications. Fig 3.4, on the facing page, shows one such respirator. It simply covers the mouth and nose, and so offers no protection for your skin or eyes. It is therefore not suitable for use where the manufacturer indicates that a material can enter your body through the skin. This information will be given in the firm's Health and Safety Data notes for that particular product.

FIRE RISK

Flammability is a major concern. When woodfinishing solvents evaporate, they form a mixture with the air which is potentially explosive. The actual concentration at which this occurs varies with each solvent, but an indication of flammability is given by the flash point. This is the temperature at which the vapour can form a flammable mixture with the air. The lower the flash point, the greater the flammability. Most spray materials have a flash point below 22°C (72°F) and this classifies them as highly flammable. Refer to the Health and Safety literature listed below for further information on handling, storing and using these materials.

SPRAYING: EXTRACTION SYSTEMS

The safest way to use sprayed materials is with some form of safe extraction system that will remove and filter out vapour and dust. The most common way of doing this is by using a spray booth. There are two basic types: dry back (see Fig 3.5 opposite) and water-washed (see page 85). They are described in detail in Chapter 9.

The main advantage of a spray booth is that overspray and solvent vapour are restricted to a small area, and their removal ensures a safe environment. The spray operator also benefits because overspray is drawn away from the operator.

Fig 3.3 Full equipment and clothing giving complete protection from hazardous particulate and vapour pollution.

Fig 3.4 A low-cost respirator with appropriate gas cartridge, conforming to the relevant British Standard.

Fig 3.5 A dry back spray booth

4 Surface Preparation

A great deal will be made of paying meticulous attention to detail when applying the range of finishes described in this book, but it must never be forgotten that, no matter how much care you take in applying polish, if the surface itself is not adequately prepared to receive it, the end result will be disappointing – or worse.

The reason for this is that a finish not only protects the surface, it also highlights any blemishes on it. This is particularly true of the gloss finishes: French polishing, for instance, quickly shows up any deficiencies in craftsmanship – its mirror-like lustre can only be achieved on a perfectly smooth ground, and even the slightest blemish will ruin the effect.

A brief explanation of optics will help to illustrate the effect. A smooth, polished surface acts as a mirror, reflecting light to our eyes so that we see a reflection of nearby objects (see Fig 4.1). Fig 4.2, overleaf, illustrates the effect of a blemish, in this case a small planing tear in the surface fibres of the wood. The blemish creates many different reflective surfaces, all at different angles to each other, and each reflects light in a different direction. The result is that the blemish scatters light and so produces a break in the otherwise perfect reflection from the rest of the surface. The problem is that sometimes these blemishes are not obviously visible until you start applying the finish, at which point they reveal themselves. In fact, the unpolished surface is not usually a good reflector of light, so you do not always notice these tiny blemishes. However, they cannot escape your sense of touch, so during surface preparation slowly run your fingers over the work without applying any pressure, and also put your eye level pretty close to that of the surface (see Fig 4.3).

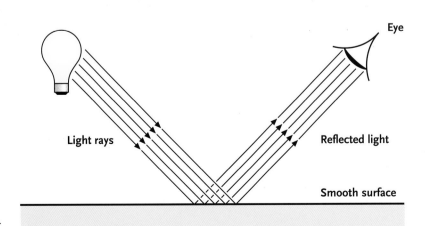

Fig 4.1 A smooth, mirror-like surface reflects light uniformly so that the eye sees perfect reflection.

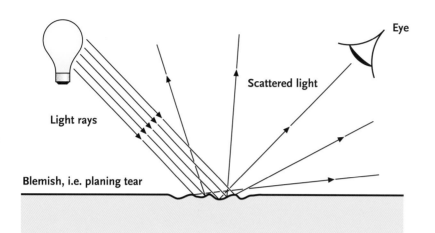

Fig 4.2 Blemishes, such as planing tears, will scatter light in all directions, making the area appear darker and duller because less light reaches the eye.

Fig 4.3 To detect blemishes, examine surfaces against the light, using a combination of touch and sight.

Looking obliquely at a low angle is more revealing than looking from directly above. The combination of sight and touch is formidable.

There is a fairly widespread misconception that a very small surface defect can somehow be masked with stain and polish, as if to 'paint' it out. While there certainly is a technique used by professional polishers to mask certain blemishes, it is generally untrue that you can paper over the cracks: they need to be removed.

SMOOTHING TOOLS

It is rare for a piece of wood to be smooth enough to polish direct from a plane iron. There are usually a number of marks caused by the plane, such as tears or undulations, due to the curved nature of jack and fore plane irons, or the occasional ridge caused by a chip in the edge of the iron. Machine-planed timber is even less likely to be suitable for polishing direct from the knives (see Fig 4.4 on the facing page).

Ripples caused by rotating plane knives

Fig 4.4 Exaggerated view of rippled effect sometimes caused by machine planing.

Bruises, marking knife lines and pencil marks, not to mention grime caused by constant handling, need to be removed. This can be done with abrasive papers, but would take a long time. There are two tools made for the job of cleaning up the work prior to staining and polishing:

SMOOTHING PLANE

The iron should be extremely sharp and set very fine, to take shavings so thin they are almost transparent. The edge of the iron should be perfectly square, with the corners slightly rounded to prevent them digging in.

On difficult timbers, where the grain is running in more than one direction, you must take extra care not to plane against the grain. This might mean changing the direction of planing to minimize the amount of tearing. Fig 4.5 shows typical grain configurations and how to plane them. Incidentally, a test of skill in the use of a plane is to prepare a piece of wood so that it is ready to polish straight from the smoothing plane.

CABINET SCRAPER

This simple but extremely effective tool seems to cause problems out of all proportion to its simplicity. Despite its name, it is a cutting, not a scraping, tool. It must produce tiny shavings, not all dust. It is made of tool steel and is thin enough to be flexible, but hard enough to take a burr on its long edges. Cabinet scrapers are produced in a variety of sizes and shapes. Fig 4.6, overleaf, shows the basic shapes:

A) Rectangular, for flat surfaces.

B) 'Goose-necked' for hollows of various radii.

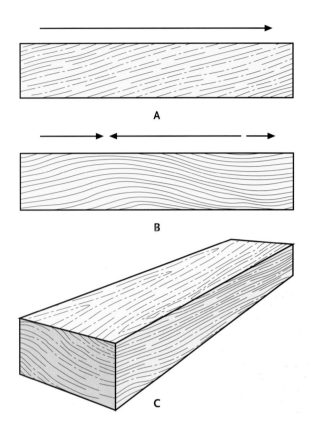

Fig 4.5 The problems of grain direction. **(A)** presents no problems in planing **(B)** shows a wavy grain, and the grain direction of **(C)** alternates in streaks across the width of the wood, making some tearing out of the grain inevitable, no matter which direction you plane the surface.

C) Rectangular, with one end for convex surfaces and the other for shallow hollows.

The latter two are clearly used for parts that a smoothing plane cannot reach.

SHARPENING A SCRAPER

Sharpening this tool requires a knack which is not difficult to achieve, provided you understand the basic principle behind the technique. In essence, you are producing an edge which is straight, square across its width and burnished smooth of any marks. This edge is

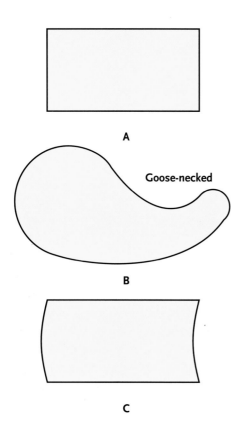

A

Goose-necked

B

C

Fig 4.6 Cabinet-scraper shapes.

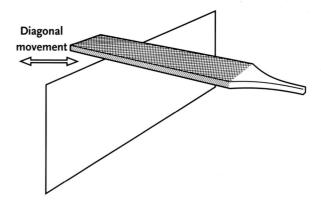

Diagonal
movement

Fig 4.7 Filing the edge of a cabinet scraper square.

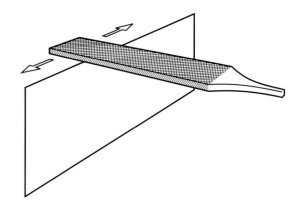

Fig 4.8 Draw-filing the edge.

then 'turned' to produce a burr, which is what actually cuts the wood.

Even a brand-new scraper needs to be sharpened. The following procedure applies to a plain rectangular scraper:

- Hold it in a vice with a long edge horizontal.

- Using a fine metal file, produce a straight edge which is square across (see Fig 4.7), then draw-file to remove marks made by the teeth (see Fig 4.8).

- Rub the edge on a fine oil- or water-stone to remove all traces of file marks (see Fig 4.9).

- There will now be a rough burr on the edge; level this off by rubbing the sides of the scraper on the stone (see Fig 4.10).

- Repeat the procedure on the other long edge.

A new burr must be made, using a 'burnisher' made of high-speed steel rod about $1/4$in (6mm) diameter, mounted in a wooden handle. The rod is held horizontal and drawn hard along each long edge once. It is then drawn along it depressed about 5° from the horizontal on both sides of the edge, to produce the burr. Repeat the process on the other long edge (see Fig 4.11), and the new scraper is now ready for use. For future sharpening, the four old burrs need to be removed first, by honing the flat faces on the fine stone.

The shaped scrapers cannot be sharpened this way. Old burrs are removed by honing and the edge is burnished ready for turning, using fine 'wet-or-dry' abrasive paper wrapped around a wooden dowel. The edges are then turned with the burnisher using the method described above.

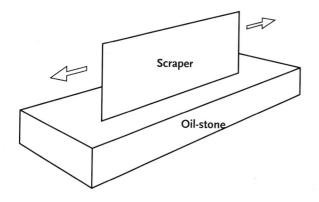

Fig 4.9 Smoothing the edge on a water- or oil-stone.

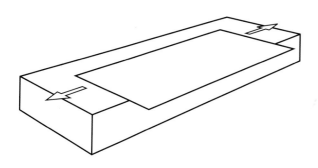

Fig 4.10 Removing the burr produced by filing the edge.

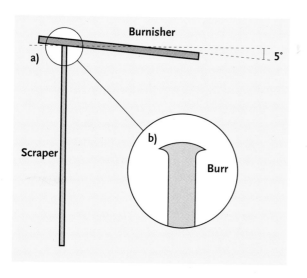

Fig 4.11 Using the burnisher to 'turn' the edge and create the cutting burr. (Detail) An exaggerated view of the edge and burr.

USING THE SCRAPER

Hold the scraper as shown in Fig 4.12, with both thumbs flexing the centre and the fingers of both hands curled around the short edges to support it. Push the blade along the surface, tilted just off the vertical so that the burr cuts. A guillotining action is needed, with the blade set slightly skew to the direction of cut, which should always be along the grain. This eases the cutting action, but also means that some of the blade will be on the wood at the ends of the stroke, so it is supported and the edge of the wood is not damaged by the scraper falling off.

If the scraper has been sharpened correctly, very fine shavings will be produced, and on very hard woods the surface will take on a sheen as it is smoothed. For very difficult grain configurations, a scraper is an alternative to the smoothing plane, as it does not tear out the fibres. In all other cases, it is used after the plane. Always take long strokes from one end of the wood to the other if possible, to prevent hollowing of the surface and to reduce the risk of marking. The scraper can get very hot, and will burn your thumbs, so wear sticking plasters to protect them.

Fig 4.12 Holding the scraper in use as a cutting tool.

ABRASIVES

On the back of abrasive paper you will see numbers and codes, which refer to the coarseness of the abrasive. The important number is the grit size, as this is the only number which is consistent across the different brands (see Fig 4.13). The higher the number, the finer the particles. For the finisher, the important grit sizes range from 150, for initial preparation, through to 320, for ultra-smooth surfaces ready for polishing. The number actually represents the size of the particles that can pass through a mesh of a given size.

Abrasive papers come in two main weights, A and C: 'A' weight paper is fairly lightweight, with closely spaced particles and thin backing paper, and is designed for hand sanding. 'C' weight is heavier-duty, with a thick backing paper and particles that are further apart. Such papers are sometimes called 'open-coat'. They are

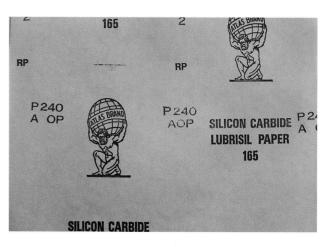

Fig 4.13 The backing paper of all abrasives provides information about the abrasive. In this case the Lubrisil paper is 'A' weight (ideal for hand sanding) and has a fine grit (240).

designed for use on sanding machines, hence their toughness. As a machine will obviously move the paper at a much faster speed than the human hand, the wider spacings of the particles are needed to reduce clogging.

There are a number of different types of abrasives in common use by woodworkers and polishers:

GLASSPAPER

Particles of ground glass are bonded onto the paper. This is not a very good abrasive, as the particles quickly lose their edge. True glasspaper is becoming less widely available.

GARNET PAPER

Ground garnet stone is the abrasive. This is a long-lasting paper, and represents very good value for money. It has a good cut on bare and polished wood, making it suitable for initial preparation of the surface and for cutting back the first coat or two of polish.

ALUMINIUM OXIDE

Also called production paper, this mineral is hard enough to use on metal. Again, it is very long lasting and good value for money.

SILICON CARBIDE

The hardest of the common abrasive papers, this comes in a waterproof version which everyone knows as 'wet-or-dry'. It is a very expensive paper, but is obtainable in grit sizes down to 1200, very useful for cutting back

TABLE 2

GRIT SIZE	GLASSPAPER SIZE	GRADE
320	–	9/0
280	–	8/0
240	–	7/0
220	00	6/0
150	0	4/0
120	1	3/0
100	1½	2/0
80	F2	0
60	M2	½
50	S2	1
30	2½	1½
24	3	2

TABLE 2 Comparison of abrasive grading codes used on the backing paper.

Fig 4.14 This mesh abrasive by Scotch is very long lasting and extremely useful for sanding shaped surfaces, or cutting back between coats of varnish.

rubber burns during French polishing. The 600 grit, used wet, is ideal for rubbing down between coats of polyurethane or yacht varnish, to produce a very fine key for subsequent coats. 800 grit and finer papers can be used to cut back French polish between bodies (see Chapter 7).

LUBRISIL

Silicon carbide again, but this paper contains its own lubricant that helps to prevent clogging. It is a great favourite of many woodturners, as its resistance to clogging makes it ideal for high-speed sanding. It is a matter of personal preference, of course, but I have not found its expense justified by its performance, and tend to stick to garnet, production and wet-or-dry.

NYLON MESH ABRASIVE PADS

A recent innovation is the appearance of nylon mesh pads impregnated with abrasive material. The grades available are purely descriptive, i.e. coarse, fine and ultra-fine. The ultra-fine grade is extremely useful for smoothing between coats of French polish and spray lacquers. See Fig 4.14.

PREPARING A SURFACE

The nature of the surface will, to a large degree, determine the best method of smoothing. For a better understanding of this, three broad categories of surface are identified below.

1. NEW, SOLID, WOOD

Use a smoothing plane initially and then finish off with the cabinet scraper. It has to be said that the scraper is not much use on softwoods, as the softness of the fibres make the surface spring under the pressure of the scraper, and virtually no cutting takes place.

For coarse-grained timbers such as oak and ash, which are to be waxed or oiled, the surface is usually suitable for taking the polish direct from the scraper blade, as it allows for a certain rustic charm. For any other finish, such timbers must be sanded using very fine grit sizes.

If a scraper has not been used, begin with a grit size of 150. Always sand with the grain and never across it, as cross-sanding always leaves scratches which show through the polish. This means extra care when sanding panelled work where adjoining members have different grain directions (i.e. rails and stiles). Fig 4.15 shows the order of sanding the members of panelled work. Any accidental cross-sanding at the joints will be eliminated later on.

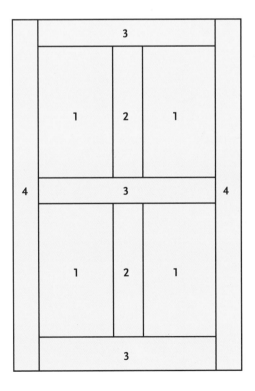

Fig 4.15 The order used in sanding panelled work.

Dust off regularly, and when the paper seems to be gliding over the surface, it is time to change to a finer grit and repeat the process. Each grade leaves its own tiny scratches, and by passing to progressively finer grits they become less. Move from 150 to 180, and then 240 grits. If the wood is particularly fine grained (e.g. sycamore or satinwood) or you are French polishing the work, finish off with 320 grit. By the time you have finished, the wood should have a definite sheen if it is smooth enough.

Always use a cork rubber on large flat surfaces, and never dwell on any one area; rather, take long strokes and work the whole surface once, and come back to start again. This way you will prevent localized hollows. See Fig 4.16.

Mouldings can present a problem, as their profiles are often rapidly destroyed by careless use of the paper. Either use a sanding block of the reverse profile, or use nylon mesh abrasive, which moulds itself to the profile.

Machine sanding of solid wood surfaces is an option, particularly with large flat ones. Chapter 2 explains the tools and protocols. Belt sanders are quite fierce and will quickly remove material. On large surfaces, a belt sander can be used instead of a smoothing plane, but if a 'fine' finish, such as French polish, is needed, the surface will not be of good enough quality. Use a cabinet scraper or orbital sander with a very fine abrasive (such as 320 grit) to prepare the surface prior to final hand sanding.

2. VENEERED WORK

Veneers are thin, making it easy to sand straight through to the groundwork beneath. There is also no need for coarse abrasives because a veneered surface will be relatively smooth. It may also be contaminated with adhesive and jointing tape residue, and so careful use of an orbital sander or hand sanding will be needed. Use a 240 grit, quickly followed by 320.

Marquetry, quartered and inlaid work will have grain running in different directions. It is not feasible to keep changing the direction of sanding, so start with 240 grit to reduce the risk of obvious cross-sanding marks showing through the final polish. Yet another problem

Fig 4.16 A cork rubber provides the best means of sanding flat surfaces evenly.

can occur when dark and light veneers are used. The grain of the light veneer tends to turn dark as dust migrates from the dark veneer. Regularly dust down and, when you have finished, a blast of compressed air will clear out the grain. Under no circumstances use a damp rag, as this will fix the dust in the grain.

3. STRIPPED SURFACES

These have already been through a process of surface preparation at least once before. This makes them different from new surfaces in several ways.

First, they will be smoother, so a fine grit such as 240 or 320 should be quite sufficient. Use a minimum amount of sanding.

Second, veneers may present a couple of problems. There may be bubbles, or lifting edges and veneer joints. These should be dealt with before continuing.

Third, during its life, the wood may have acquired scratches and dents. You have to decide whether or not you can live with them. Unless they are disfiguring or will prevent you attaining the finish you require, it may be best to leave them. There is little point using filler in very shallow depressions, as it is always detectable (and may look worse than the damage) and will probably fall out anyway. Shallow dents can be steamed out as described below.

SURFACE BLEMISHES

There may be blemishes that need to be filled or steamed out. The material used as a filler will depend

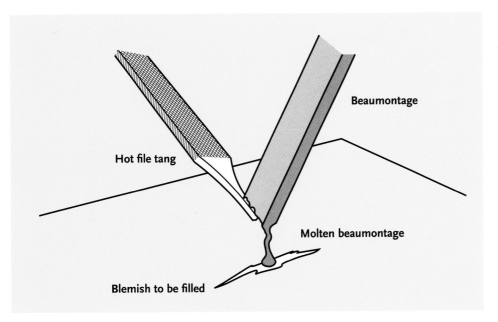

Hot file tang

Beaumontage

Molten beaumontage

Blemish to be filled

Fig 4.17 Melting wax or shellac filler into a deep blemish.

on the finish you intend to use, and you need to be mindful of compatibility with the intended finish.

WAX AND SHELLAC FILLER STICKS

If the wood is to be waxed, use a coloured wax stick, which you can make yourself (see Chapter 16). The wax is melted into the blemish using the tang of a file heated by a spirit burner (see Fig 4.17). For French polish, a shellac stick is melted into the blemish in a similar way. In both cases, the sticks are made in a range of colours to match that of the stained surface, and the blemish is filled proud of the surface. When it has hardened, level it with a sharp chisel. Wax and shellac stopping are often referred to as beaumontage. You may prefer to carry out this filling stage after staining, when it will be easier to match the colour to the stain; this is fine, but take care when levelling, as it is too easy to cut through the stain.

Wax and shellac fillers are not compatible with synthetic spray lacquers, as their solvent will simply dissolve the filler. A wax filler is also not suitable under solvent-based varnishes.

PROPRIETARY FILLERS

Proprietary wood fillers are available in a range of colours to match that of the item, but you must check compatibility with your intended finish. Manufacturers of commercial woodfinishing products usually match

filler to finish in their product lists. They are usually soft and paste-like for application by spatula. Some dry by evaporation of a solvent, while others harden by catalytic action and are ideal for filling areas close to the edge of the work. They can be smoothed off by sanding prior to staining the work, so their colour needs to match the finished product as closely as possible.

STEAMING

Minor depressions that are too shallow to fill (the beaumontage will fall out) can usually be steamed out before staining. Place a clean wet cloth over the patch and press a hot clothes iron on to it; the steam generated will be forced into the compressed fibres, causing them to swell. Two or three attempts may be needed. Afterwards, when the area has dried, re-sand the surface with very fine abrasive paper.

FINAL PREPARATIONS

If you intend to use a water-based stain, the surface needs to be moistened with warm water and allowed to dry, to forestall any tendency for the stain to swell the fibres of the wood . By wetting at this stage, allowing the fibres to swell, and then sanding with a 320 grit paper, there will be little or no swelling after the stain is applied, when you would be unable to cut back the raised fibres, at least not without removing the colour. (See the following chapter, Staining and Bleaching.)

5 Staining and Bleaching

There are several reasons why you will want to change the colour of wood. Disguising inferior wood to make it appear rather better is an obvious reason, but the more usual reasons include:

- **UNIFORMITY** As it is a natural material, wood will vary in colour, texture and figure. This is part of its charm. It can also cause a problem in that wood used from different sources, or even different parts of the same tree, may vary significantly. This lack of uniformity may spoil the look of the work in some circumstances, so staining or bleaching is a legitimate means of gaining uniformity.

- **DISGUISE** You may wish to make a perfectly good piece of wood resemble a different species. There is absolutely nothing wrong with this. For example, beech is the ideal wood for chair frames. It is hard, very close grained and incredibly boring to look at. By staining it to resemble, say, mahogany, walnut, or oak, you are making it more interesting to view, so that beech dining chairs can be made to match a mahogany dining table.

- **MATCHING AND BLENDING** This is probably the most difficult of colouring tasks. New wood used in a repair will need to be coloured to match the old, or a new piece of furniture may need to be coloured to blend in with other items of furniture or a room's colour scheme.

- **PROTECTION** In Chapter 12, the use of preservative materials is discussed in detail. The one thing common to all those designed for exterior use is that they are heavily coloured with special chemicals that protect the wood from the considerable damaging effects of the sun's ultraviolet (UV) light.

DYEING MATERIALS

In theory, any coloured material could be employed to stain wood, and there are a number of exotic examples used in the furniture restoration trade. The choice of staining material may be determined by the finish you intend to apply over it. In certain circumstances, the finish may be incompatible with the stain.

The staining material may also be included in the finish itself, such as polyurethane stain varnish. The advantage of this is that a separate staining process is not needed, and so saves time. In commercial finishing, the spray lacquer itself may be coloured. Because it forms a heavily coloured film over the surface, the wood's figure is often masked and, worse still, veneer inlays of contrasting colour are effectively lost.

Another problem with these materials is that if they are damaged the colour of the wood shows through. Typically, this is considerably lighter than the varnish or lacquer. This makes the damage unsightly and difficult to repair without it being obvious.

This chapter looks at staining – or dyeing – materials that do not form part of the finish itself. Coloured varnishes and lacquers are applied in the same way as their clear versions (see Chapters 8 and 9). Colouring materials are also used to correct colour casts and errors, and for colour matching. These are discussed in detail in Chapters 9 and 10.

The following descriptions provide general information on the commonly used, and readily available, staining materials in use. As manufacturers vary in terms of the nature and range of specific products, you need to refer to their technical literature for the properties of specific products, but the following gives a good overview of the main types.

OIL STAINS (NAPHTHA STAINS)

These are based on white spirit as the solvent, with a binder to hold the colour in the wood once the solvent has dried. Only one coat, or at most two, should be used because successive coats produce a surface film which looks varnished; also, you run the risk of dissolving the binder and lifting the colour out of the wood, creating a patchy effect – this is especially true if you have not allowed it to dry thoroughly.

Having said that, oil stains have some extremely attractive features, which is why they are a commercial success: they are relatively easy to use, producing a generally uniform colour; they have good penetration and coverage, and they are designed to be applied by brush or pad. Everyone has used them at some time or other, and the names of Colron, Blackfriars, Fiddes and Rustin's are familiar names.

If you intend to use these stains with a wax or varnish finish take extra care in ensuring that the dye has dried completely as there is a risk of 'bleed' – the solvent in the finish may soften and lift the colour. Oil polishing should not be attempted with this type of dye as bleed is a serious risk.

WATER-BASED DYES

These dyes are a relatively recent addition to the wood-colouring kit. A distinction is made here between the traditional water dyes described later and the latest generation of wood dyes that have been designed as a 'solvent-free' alternative to naphtha and spirit dyes. They were developed partly in response to changes in health and safety regulations (most notably COSHH) which meant that manufacturers and users needed to take account of hazards and risks associated with materials. These dyes are safer because they are not based on volatile and flammable solvents.

Because they are water-based, there is the risk of the grain raising (as described in Chapter 4), even though they contain an anti-grain-raising ingredient. However, you should carry out the sand-wet-sand method before using these stains to reduce the risk of further grain raising, as this is still a possibility. They are applied by brush or pad and are compatible with all finishes.

NGR STAINS

Non-grain-raising (NGR) stains are based on highly volatile solvents. They dry within an hour usually and can be applied by pad or brush. An added bonus is that they can also be added to French polish or cellulose lacquers for colour correction or matching (see Chapters 9 and 10). Colour depth can be increased by applying more coats after allowing the previous coat to dry. The colour can also be weakened by thinning with NGR thinners or methylated spirits (meths).

NON-STRIKE STAINS

These are strictly meant for commercial production work where speed and consistency is required. They are sprayed onto the wood surface and dry within minutes, which makes them impractical to apply by brush or pad because this would result in tidemarks. Multiple coats will deepen the colour, so weaken the colour by thinning with cellulose thinners. These stains can also be mixed with French polish or cellulose lacquers, for colour-matching and correction.

MATCHING TINTS AND DYES

Designed to be used in commercial production work, these dyes are used for colour matching and correction. Some products are pre-mixed with cellulose lacquer, for example, to be sprayed onto absorbent wood to ensure an even colour where normal dyes would result in patchiness. Tinting dyes are very concentrated and a small amount is mixed with cellulose lacquer or French polish for matching and correcting colour errors.

Before buying these materials, check they are compatible with the intended finish.

ANILINE DYES

Invented in Germany in the nineteenth century, these chemicals produce an enormous range of colours. They can be bought in powder or liquid form as single colours (e.g. red, blue, green, yellow) or as specific 'wood' colours. There are two varieties: one uses meths as the solvent, the other uses water, but unfortunately, they are not light-fast in the presence of strong sunlight. They are used mostly by furniture restorers where there is a need to match new components to the original by mixing colours, for an exact colour match.

Both forms are highly soluble in their respective solvents, and are extremely powerful colouring agents. A teaspoon of powder to a pint (500ml) of solvent will produce quite a strong colour. If you are mixing your own colour, it is better to make up separate colour solutions first and mix them. The depth of colour is controlled, as you might expect, by altering the concentration of the solution. Of course, never mix water- and spirit-based dyes.

Water-based anilines are compatible with all finishes and penetrate the wood, but spirit dyes may be lifted by French polish (as it is meths-based). If applied heavily, they will mask the wood surface. Add a dash of ammonia to water anilines, to break down the surface tension and so aid penetration of the wood.

VANDYKE CRYSTALS

This is a traditional wood dye used by restorers. The crystals are water-soluble and produce a basic chestnut brown traditionally used on walnut and oak, but it is also effective in producing a warm brown mahogany. According to concentration, the depth of colour can be varied from honey to black. The crystals do not dissolve easily, but the following method will make the job easier:

Mix the crystals to a paste with hot water, and then gradually add more hot water to dissolve. Add a dash of ammonia to aid penetration. Test the colour and adjust the concentration as necessary. Store the stain in a wide-necked jar. As the water cools, some of the crystals come out of the solution and form a sediment at the bottom. This sediment can be retrieved later and dissolved in more hot water.

If the stain is rubbed on panelling as a thin paste, a shading effect can be created, similar to old patinated surfaces, by rubbing away from the centre into the edges where the panel meets the frame, using a wrung-out wet cloth. Use the same technique of rubbing away from the centre to create 'wear' on chair and table rails.

CHEMICAL STAINS

Staining can be achieved with a number of chemicals which react with certain substances in the wood itself. Not all woods will respond, and even those that do may not stain evenly, because the action depends very much on the concentration of chemicals (notably tannic acid) present in the wood. The colour of the chemical stain bears no relation to the final colour achieved. In other words, the effect of these staining materials is much less predictable. The most commonly used chemicals and their actions are:

BICHROMATE OF POTASH This is orange in colour; a solution of 2oz (50g) in a pint (500ml) of warm water will turn true mahogany a red/brown and oak a warm, mellow brown.

IRON SALTS In weak solutions these give a silvery tone to oak, and may also be used to kill the redness of mahogany if you want to stain it to resemble walnut. They produce a greyish tone on sycamore to create 'harewood' (especially useful in marquetry). In a strong solution, iron salts will turn oak inky-black; the black discolouration around iron nails and screws in external oak timbers is the result of iron stains. Steep iron nails in white vinegar overnight and decant the liquid as a stock solution of iron acetate.

AMMONIA The strongest solution available is called 'point eight eighty' (0.880), and is 35% ammonia. On its own, the 35% solution creates only a slight darkening of oak, but if oak is exposed to the ammonia fumes, the effect is dramatic as it darkens progressively, and eventually turns a deep grey-black. This method of exposing oak to ammonia vapour is called 'fuming'. The product is 'fumed oak', which has the characteristic charcoal-grey colour, with the medullary rays showing up as a dark silver-grey colour, which make it resemble ancient oak. Conventional wood dyes cannot recreate the colour of ancient oak that has darkened after centuries of exposure to air and its pollutants.

Fuming is unpleasant work and you will need to take precautions to protect yourself from the fumes. Place the item to be fumed beneath an upturned plastic fishtank (or similar) with a saucer or two of the ammonia solution. You can observe the action of the ammonia without being exposed to the fumes for any length of time. Observe the colour change and remove the item once it has reached the colour you want.

Since 0.880 ammonia is difficult to find, household ammonia will do the trick, although it will obviously take longer.

OTHER STRONG ALKALIS Caustic soda, washing soda and other strong alkalis will darken oak, mahogany and other hardwoods, which is one reason for not using caustic stripping on these timbers. 1oz to a pint (25g to 500ml) of clean water is a good stock solution, which can be strengthened or diluted as necessary.

MIXING AND TESTING STAINS

The other great thing about proprietary brands of wood dyes is that they are produced in standard colours, and each brand name has its own colour chart. They are produced to very high standards of quality that ensure consistent colour reproduction between batches. Choose carefully, however, as the samples on colour cards are usually on thin plywood or pine, which is initially white. You must always take into account (with all stains, in fact) that the final colour will be modified by that of the wood. You may find that a 'walnut' stain looks better on mahogany than a 'mahogany' stain.

You should test the colour before committing it to the work in hand. In fact, this is a general rule for all staining work. You can do this by trying it on leftover pieces of wood of the same species. If this is not possible, try an inconspicuous area of the work.

APPLYING STAINS

Staining materials can be applied in one of three ways: brush, pad or spray. The subject of spraying is considered in detail in Chapter 9. This chapter describes the other two methods of application.

Fig 5.1 Staining by brush. Note the slight overlap between strokes to ensure full coverage.

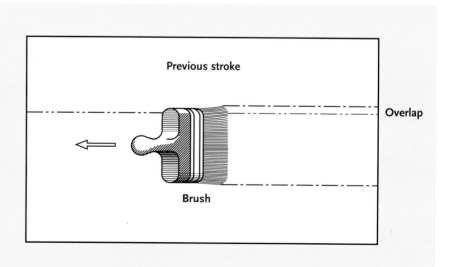

TIP BOX
Wear rubber gloves and protect yourself from splashes. Many materials used for staining wood are irritants, or worse, and there is at the very least a high risk of contact dermatitis.

BRUSH METHOD

- Decant the stain into a wide-necked container. If you are using solvent-based stains (i.e. not water-based) the container should not be plastic as this may be softened or dissolved by the solvent, with the inevitable leakage of the stain.

- Use paintbrushes reserved solely for stains. The problem with brushes that have been used with paint or varnish is that they can contaminate the surface with old residue of paint or varnish.

- Charge the brush, and squeeze out surplus from the bristle tips by pressing against the side of the container. On large flat areas such as table tops, apply the stain in straight strokes along the grain, working from the edge furthest away from you and gradually moving towards you.

- Overlap the strokes slightly, as shown in Fig 5.1 on the facing page, so that only one 'live' edge is kept open (to prevent tidemarks) and recharge the brush as needed. When the whole surface has been covered, take a clean, lint-free rag, dip it into the stain and thoroughly wring it out. Form the rag into a pad and wipe over the work along the grain in straight strokes, to even out the colour. Allow to dry.

If you are using water- or spirit-based stains, the work can be recoated to darken the shade, once the first coat has dried.

The work should be broken down into manageable sections. Do not try to complete a large piece all at once, as the stain will dry before you can even it out. On a table, for example, treat the top as one section, the legs as another, and so on.

Carving and intricate mouldings may need a stabbing action with the brush to ensure that no spots are missed. If this does happen, missed areas can be touched up with a pencil brush.

PAD METHOD

This method can really only be used satisfactorily on flat surfaces. Mouldings, carvings and panelled work need the brush method. Fold some upholstery wadding into a ball, wrap it in a clean, lint-free cotton cloth and flatten the face to form the pad, as shown in Fig 5.2.

Dip the pad into the stain and wait as it is drawn up into the wadding. After a few moments, squeeze the

Fig 5.2 The pad used to apply stain. The cloth is tightly wrapped around the wadding to keep it firm for controlled application of the stain.

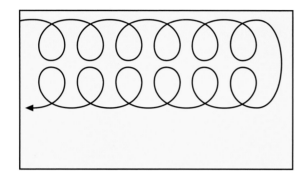

Fig 5.3 Use a circular path when first applying the stain, to force it into the surface pores.

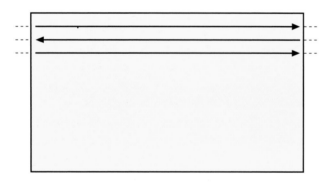

Fig 5.4 Finish off with straight strokes to even out the colour distribution.

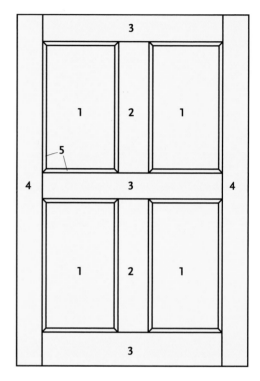

Fig 5.5 Staining panelled work. The correct sequence will ensure even coverage 1) panels 2) muntins 3) rails 4) stiles 5) mouldings.

pad against the side to force out surplus stain, and then work the stain over the surface in a circular motion, as shown in Fig 5.3. Apply little or no pressure at first, as the stain will flow freely onto the work, and gradually increase pressure as it dries out. Recharge the pad if necessary. Finish off by working along the grain as in Fig 5.4, to eliminate the circular paths and to even out the colour.

STAINING PANELLED WORK

Figure 5.5 shows the order in which to stain the components of panelled work. This approach reduces the risk of tidemarks.

BLEACHING WOOD

There are many occasions where you may want to lighten the colour of the wood rather than darken it. This will involve bleaching the surface by chemical action, and the following are circumstances where this will be needed:

- To remove unsightly blemish stains such as dark water marks, ink stains, iron stains in oak.

- To lighten the overall colour of the wood – e.g. to produce a 'blond oak' – or to bleach out a previously applied colour-stain or dye, when it is too dark.

Oxalic acid or 20 vol. hydrogen peroxide should deal with some of the unsightly dark stains described in the first bullet point, but a very dramatic lightening of a surface will require the use of a two-part wood bleach.

OXALIC ACID

Oxalic acid is a toxic, crystalline organic compound that is best obtained through commercial woodfinish suppliers. Woodwork journals are the best source of addresses. Since it is a toxic compound, take appropriate measures to protect yourself and others. This includes keeping the stuff in well-labelled containers, indicating that it is toxic, and under lock and key. You must also protect yourself while using the acid, by wearing rubber gloves and eye-protectors. While it is not strongly corrosive, it is nevertheless an irritant, and it is wise not to handle it with unprotected skin.

Make up a solution of approximately 2oz in a pint (50g in 500ml) of warm water, sponge over the discoloured area (which, of course, has been stripped of any kind of finish) and allow to dry thoroughly. You may find a whitish deposit on the surface when it dries. This is crystals of oxalic acid, which can be brushed off, wearing a mask to avoid inhaling the crystals. Residual acid in the wood has to be neutralised with a solution of 1oz borax in a pint (25g in 500ml) of warm water,

sponged on and allowed to dry. Afterwards, the surface will be a little fuzzy, due to raised grain, so give a very light sand before staining and finishing. Fig 5.6 shows before and after photographs, showing the effect of oxalic acid on an ink stain. You can repeat the process over a stubborn stain.

WEAK HYDROGEN PEROXIDE

20 vol. hydrogen peroxide is readily bought over the counter at any pharmacy, as it is a weak solution. Hydrogen peroxide is chemically unstable, readily decomposing to water as it releases oxygen. It is a strong oxidizing agent. The term 'vol.' refers to the volume of oxygen it generates. A 20 vol. solution can generate 20 times its own volume of oxygen. Branded wood-bleaches usually have 100 vol. solution – i.e. it can produce 100 times its own volume of oxygen, or is five times stronger than 20 vol. The released oxygen does the bleaching and the real beauty of this is that there is no residue, as water is all that remains.

The breakdown of peroxide is accelerated by contact with metal, organic compounds or alkaline materials. This means that you must wear protective clothing, including rubber gloves, and decant the peroxide into a plastic, glass or ceramic container. Do not pour leftover peroxide back into its original container as this will contaminate the remaining peroxide and cause it to decompose.

Fig 5.6 Before and after view of an ink stain bleached out with oxalic acid.

Sponge the peroxide over the stained area and wait for it to dry before judging its effectiveness. Any fuzziness in the surface can be lightly sanded when dry. Repeat the process on stubborn stains.

TWO-PART WOOD BLEACH

As their name implies, two-part bleaches are made up of two chemicals. One is a strong solution of hydrogen peroxide, and the other is a strong alkali, usually a 2% caustic soda solution.

The hydrogen peroxide does the bleaching by releasing oxygen as it breaks down by chemical reaction, but the process is slow, so an activator is required to speed it up. This is the purpose of the caustic soda solution. Peroxide rapidly breaks down if exposed to alkaline materials. As the newly generated oxygen attacks the chemicals in the wood, it changes them and removes their colour.

You can make up your own two-part bleach using peroxide available over the counter at pharmacists, but this is a weak solution of 20 or 30 vol. Stronger solutions of peroxide, with more powerful bleaching action, can be bought from hairdressing suppliers, who sell it in strengths up to 60 vol. This is a cost-effective way of buying it. For the alkaline solution in your home-made two-part bleach, use sodium bicarbonate solution, say a tablespoon to a pint (500ml) of warm water.

Proprietary wood bleaches usually use 100 vol hydrogen peroxide, which is a very strong and corrosive oxidizing agent, leading to unpleasant chemical burns if it is allowed to get onto your skin. Safe storage is essential. It is supplied in plastic bottles, tightly stoppered, and it should be stored like this in its original container.

- Only open it when you need to use it. The vapour above the liquid has a high concentration of oxygen.

- Store the wood bleach in a dark, cool place, preferably in a metal cabinet designed specifically for the storage of chemicals.

- Over time, peroxide breaks down naturally and may cause the container to 'blow' – i.e. swell out with the pressure of the released oxygen. If that happens, slowly release the cap to relieve the pressure before opening it completely.

- The caustic soda solution is quite weak, but still represents a hazard as a corrosive material. This should be stored in its original container also, and under lock and key in a chemical storage cabinet.

- Use synthetic bristle brushes, as true bristle will disintegrate, and have separate brushes for the peroxide and caustic soda solutions, to prevent contamination and chemical reaction by mixing the two on the same brush. Decant each solution into separate and labelled plastic, glass, or ceramic containers, and discard unused solutions, as they may be contaminated. If you pour them back into their respective containers, the resulting chemical reaction may cause the container to explode. Never use metal containers, as both solutions will react with the metal.

Two-part bleach should be applied in the following way:

1. Brush the first (alkaline) solution over the wood, taking care not to flood it, and leave for a few minutes. On some hardwoods the colour may darken alarmingly, but this is normal and it will lighten again when the peroxide is applied.

2. Brush the second solution over the wood and leave to dry. This is the hydrogen peroxide, and it may froth after a minute or so. Again, this is quite normal, and is the result of the oxygen being released from the peroxide.

3. Leave the work to dry out, which should take about a day. The wood will be furry due to raised grain, and there may be the odd water mark. Gently wash down with a weak solution of white vinegar to neutralize the alkaline residue left by the caustic soda, and leave to dry for another day or so. Gently sand smooth with a 320 grit paper, not too deeply, as bleaching does not penetrate very far. If the work is not light enough, repeat the bleaching process.

PIGMENTS

Pigments are coloured powders that do not dissolve in a liquid; in this respect they are fundamentally different to stains. When stirred into a liquid, the powders remain suspended for a while before settling to the bottom of the container as shown in Fig 5.7. Their role in woodfinishing is limited, but those uses to which they are put cannot be fulfilled by true stains. For example, if raw umber (which is a dirty, greeny grey) is mixed with wax polish used on pine, it helps create an antique effect by collecting in crevices and giving the surface a general powdery look that normally comes with age. Because pigments lie on the surface of wood, they do give a granular effect worth experimenting with. However, it is best to restrict your colours to the so-called earth pigments. The use of pigments is described in later chapters.

Fig 5.7 This shows the difference between stains and pigments. A stain will dissolve in its solvent (left), while pigments will not dissolve, but will be suspended in the liquid, gradually settling out on the bottom of the container (right).

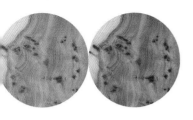

Wax and Oil Polishing

Wax and oil are among the oldest forms of wood finishes and this has earned them their place as the most 'natural' and aesthetically pleasing of the traditional finishes. Wax and oil represent good craftsmanship, natural beauty and a reaction to the 'evils' of mass production. This was certainly the view of the furniture makers and designers of the Arts and Crafts movement in the nineteenth century. Their view was that there had been a debasement of craftsmanship, and so they harked back to an earlier age devoid of machinery but rich in the high values placed on 'honest' hand craftsmanship, i.e. the Middle Ages. Their work was characterized by the almost exclusive use of home-grown timbers, and was simply designed and beautifully constructed, using classical cabinetmaking techniques. The pieces were frequently left unfinished, oiled or waxed.

This is still the image of waxing and oiling, but the same charge can be levelled against them as was made against the indiscriminate use of French polish towards the end of the nineteenth century and the beginning of the twentieth. Wax and oil polishes are just as capable of indiscriminate and inappropriate application. 'Rustic' timbers such as oak look well under the low lustre of oil and wax, which leave the surface with a texture and tactile quality that is so admired; however, many of the highly figured and richly coloured woods need to be brought alive by the optical properties of 'hard' finishes such as French polish or cellulose lacquer.

Amongst the most common errors is to attempt to dress varnished, French polished, or lacquered furniture with beeswax or furniture oil. All that results from this is a greasy build-up which eventually dulls and masks the surface, as it attracts dust and other pollutants in the air.

While some products on the market are specifically designed to be used on these 'hard' finishes, they are of special formulation, and should be used very sparingly and not very often. Beeswax polish and the various furniture oils such as Danish oil, tung oil and linseed oil, are wood finishes in their own right, and are not designed to be used with anything else.

Before describing the materials involved, Table 3 compares and contrasts the advantages and disadvantages of wax and oil polishes.

TABLE 3

QUALITIES	WAX	OIL
Easy to apply	Yes	Yes
Durability	Low	High
Heat and water resistance	Low	High
Renewability and revival	Yes	Yes

The inevitable conclusions drawn from the information in Table 3 are:

- As they are easy to apply, a high level of practical skills is not required to apply these polishes.

- Wax polish is vulnerable and therefore not suitable for projects subject to a great deal of wear or exposure to heat and moisture.

- Oil is particularly resistant to moisture and hot crockery and can therefore be used on dining tables, coffee tables, etc.

- Both forms of polish are easily renewed or revived by the application of another coat.

SURFACE PREPARATION: BURNISHING

The surface preparation procedures described in Chapter 4 should be used. If a scraper has been used on oak, polishing can take place without the need for sanding. There is a useful technique called burnishing, which helps to give hardwoods an initial sheen by compressing the surface wood fibres.

The burnisher is made from another piece of hardwood, usually beech, which is very hard and close grained. Its shape is shown in Fig 6.1, and Fig 6.2 shows the burnisher in use. By rubbing the rounded edge of the tool along the grain with as much pressure as you and the furniture can stand, the surface fibres are compressed, packing them tightly and creating a sheen. This technique is an old one and while not obligatory, it does help to build up the shine quickly.

Fig 6.2 Using the burnisher – this is hard work, but worth the effort.

Softwoods such as pine will not burnish too well, and the pressure may cause unwanted indentations.

WAX POLISHING

Recipes for making wax polishes are given in Chapter 16. They consist of a wax dissolved in a solvent such as turpentine or white spirit. Some formulations rely on a more volatile liquid, toluene, but their extended use in unventilated areas is not recommended without the use of a mask fitted with a fume removing cartridge. Their particular advantage is the speed with which the solvent evaporates. A wax polish cannot do its job properly until the solvent has all evaporated and only the wax itself remains on the surface. Friction is then used to soften and distribute the wax as a smooth, thin, lustrous coat.

COMMONLY USED WAXES

A number of different waxes are used, either singly or, more commonly, in combination.

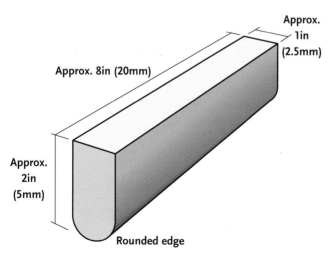

Approx. 8in (20mm)

Approx. 1in (2.5mm)

Approx. 2in (5mm)

Rounded edge

Fig 6.1 A hardwood burnisher. Note the rounded edge to prevent it digging into the surface and helping to increase the pressure over a smaller area.

BEESWAX

This is the best known and most highly regarded of the polishing waxes and its association with something so obviously natural has given rise to its reputation for representing traditional craft values. It has to be said that the pungent smell of pure turpentine with the sweet, honey smell of beeswax is irresistible.

Despite its high reputation, beeswax does have a drawback or two. There is still only one way to obtain the wax and this makes it expensive, even when you consider the highly commercialized way in which bees are 'farmed' to produce honey. Also, the wax tends to become a little tacky in warm environments. This may not be immediately apparent in a block of the stuff, but as a thin layer on furniture it will fingermark easily, and attract dust.

The wax is available in blocks or small pellets, and may be white (purified wax) or yellow (natural) in colour (see Fig 6.3).

CARNAUBA WAX

This wax forms the outer, shiny skin of the leaves of a Brazilian palm. It is very hard and brittle, like home-made toffee, so much so that it is rarely used on its own. A traditionally made beeswax polish can be improved by adding 10% carnauba wax. This has two effects on the properties of the polish. First, it stiffens it, making it a little more durable and harder when dry. Second, because of its hardness carnauba wax produces a deeper sheen than beeswax, so a mixture of the two will bring about an enhanced lustre.

PARAFFIN WAX

Candle wax, as it is commonly called, does not have too much to commend itself as a polish, but may be used in cheaper polishes to make the blend less expensive. It can also be used blended with beeswax or carnauba wax to make wax filler (see Chapter 4).

JAPAN WAX

A very expensive blend of vegetable waxes, this has exceptional properties and is found in the best traditionally blended wax polishes. You would not normally keep this in your workshop unless intending to make your own polish, although you can use it to make wax filler.

SYNTHETIC WAX

The best known is silicone wax. Synthetic waxes form the basis of many modern formulations of wax polishes. The silicones in particular have the property of imparting a very high sheen for relatively little effort. The problem, however, is that they create a high build-up and may even trap dust between the layers during each application. Eventually, instead of improving the shine, the surface begins to go dull and patchy. There is little or no place for these in the traditional polishers' toolkit, and its value lies in the commercial production of polish sprays and pastes.

WAX PASTES AND CREAMS

The stiffer pastes are produced by simply dissolving the wax in a suitable solvent, i.e. turpentine or white spirit. The wax content is, in proportionate terms, very high.

The consistency of the paste can be varied by altering the relative amounts of solvent and wax. The higher the wax content, the stiffer the paste. For the

Fig 6.3 Beeswax (left block), raw carnauba wax (right lower block) and purified carnauba wax (right upper block).

first application or so, onto bare wood, the paste ought to be fairly soft, say the consistency of butter on a warm day, as it can then be spread more easily and forced into the pores of the wood, sealing it more effectively. Subsequent applications can be made with a stiff paste, which tends to buff up more easily.

Wax creams are rather different. They are made by emulsifying the wax and solvent mixture in water, and consequently have a much lower wax content, by proportion, than will be found in a wax paste. They are not designed to be used as a finish in their own right, but as a dressing over a hard finish such as French polish, to improve lustre and provide a little additional protection. Because they also contain water and an emulsifying agent, wax creams will have an additional cleaning action on the surface. The consistency of a cream will vary in stiffness from very liquid to the consistency of cosmetic cold cream. Creams are mentioned here only to distinguish them from genuine wax polish, as there tends to be considerable confusion about the difference between the two.

There is little merit in making your own polish – other than the satisfaction of doing so – as there are so many good proprietary products available. Nevertheless, anyone who has any interest in the subject will usually want to experiment. Recipes and methods of making can be found in Chapter 16. The exception to this is antique or distressing wax, which needs to be made up as required (see later).

COLD WAX POLISHING

Wax polish is usually applied cold directly from its container, but a method of using warm, liquefied polish will be described later as it has some advantages.

You will find it helpful to seal the surface of softwoods and the more open-grained hardwoods, such as oak or ash, with a coat of transparent French polish. This can be applied sparingly with a brush and then allowed to dry for a couple of hours. By sealing the wood first, you will save on the amount of polish needed and build up the sheen quickly. Using the warm waxing method will do this also, but requires more wax.

Apply the wax with mutton cloth (stockinette), using a circular motion and forcing it into the grain. Finish off with straight strokes along the grain. Leave the polish to dry for at least an hour, longer if possible, before buffing vigorously along the grain with a new piece of mutton cloth. Alternatively, wrap a piece of terry towelling around a brick and rub along the grain. This is an excellent method for large flat surfaces (see Fig 6.4, below).

On heavily carved work, the polish should be applied with a soft-bristled shoe brush and allowed to dry before buffing with a clean brush. The main thing to remember is to avoid accumulations of wax in the corners and quirks, as once they dry there, dust and grime begin to build up. Finish off by buffing with a soft, lint-free cloth.

How many coats of wax should be applied? Waxing produces a better finish with time. Initially, two or three applications will produce an acceptable surface, but as time goes on and more applications of wax are made over a period of years, the wood surface takes on a warm, mellow glow. It cannot be produced immediately, although hot waxing will go a long way towards it.

Fig 6.4 Burnishing a waxed surface with an old towel wrapped around a brick or wooden block.

WARM WAX POLISHING

This method uses a lot of wax as the polish is applied molten and with a paintbrush over the work, then allowed to harden before remelting with a hot air gun and forced into the surface with hessian or similar open-weave cloth. The method does have a number of benefits, though. The heat aids penetration, and so the wax is driven deep into the surface. This in turn creates a more immediate effect of mellowness and age; this effect cannot be created with cold wax, which does not penetrate so deeply. The method is ideal for stripped pine furniture or doors, and if antiquing or distressing wax polish is used the ageing effect is dramatic. Once the solvent has evaporated, there remains a pleasant honey odour and a deep, mellow sheen. **N.B.** This method is not suitable for a toluene-based wax polish, because the fumes are so dangerous.

Melt the wax polish using a double-boiler arrangement, as shown in Fig 6.5. Boil the water in the pan first, then turn off the heat. Only then do you place the inner container with the wax polish in the pan. This removes the risk of fire. The polish will melt quite quickly and you can add a small amount of white spirit or pure turpentine to make it more fluid when you brush it into the work. There will be a build-up of solvent fumes because of the heat, so make sure there is plenty of ventilation.

Apply the liquid wax to the wood with a clean paintbrush, spreading it out well. The wax will begin to solidify quickly as it cools, making it hard to brush it out. It is not imperative to get 100% coverage of the area, as the next stage in the process will achieve that. In fact, it is better to miss some of the area, otherwise there will be too much wax and the rubbing cloth will become clogged and useless.

Allow to dry for at least an hour, to ensure that most of the solvent has evaporated. Use the hot air gun – placed not too close to the surface as it may scorch it or ignite the wax – to melt small areas of wax, at the same time rubbing vigorously with open-weave hessian. Close-weaved cloth is useless for this work, because it clogs quickly and will not generate the friction needed. As each area is completed, move on to the next until the whole surface has been burnished.

You will find that the hessian will become clogged with wax, and it is necessary to refold it at regular intervals to present a clear surface. On large work, you may need to replace the hessian as it becomes totally saturated with wax.

Afterwards, lay the wrung-out hessian outside to dry before disposing of it. Wet and full of wax, they represent a major fire risk. You can attempt to recover some of the wax by dissolving it in a little white spirit or pure turpentine. The safest way of disposing of old waxing cloths is by incineration.

SPRAY WAX POLISH

Waxing is quite labour-intensive, but the time and cost of waxing in production work can be reduced if the wax is sprayed onto the work. A number of manufacturers have formulated wax polishes that can be sprayed onto the work. These waxes often incorporate colour, so staining and waxing is achieved in one action. After applying a sprayed coat, allow to dry before buffing by

Fig 6.5 Double boiler arrangement for melting wax polish.

hand. If a deeper colour or sheen is required, a second sprayed coat can be applied.

Special wax-spray equipment is needed and precautions against overspray (see Chapter 9), such as the use of a spray booth, should be observed. Personal protective equipment needs to be worn by the operator to prevent risk to health. Some formulations are based on toluene while others are water-borne suspensions of wax. Chapter 9 looks at the techniques of spraying which also apply to the use of these waxes.

These products are not suitable for the home or small workshop partly because of the investment in equipment that is required, and partly because of the hazardous nature of the technique, but spray polish can also be applied by hand, using a cloth or brush, allowed to dry and then buffed.

STAINING WAX

Staining waxes are the DIY equivalent to the spray wax system. They can be bought in small quantities and are applied with a cloth, rubbing along the grain direction, as if you were applying a wood dye. They are ideal for use on items that will not be handled much, such as panelling.

DISTRESSING OR ANTIQUE WAX

Make your own distressing or antiquing wax polish as each job demands. The polish is coloured with earth pigments such as raw umber, burnt umber, lamp black, raw sienna, burnt sienna. They are not staining waxes in the way of those products described above.

A distressing wax does not dye the wood, it deposits pigment in the grain, surface blemishes, and in the angles of moulded work (see Chapter 4). It imparts a colour cast of its own and the intention is that it should simulate age, by giving a very granular look to the surface. Use of distressing wax is not an uncommon practice, and it can be very effective if it is used judiciously. Apart from giving a general colouring to the surface, the pigment that tends to become lodged in the corners of mouldings and in other corners,

Fig 6.6 The effect of a distressing wax on new pine – it simulates old wood.

suggests the build-up of dirt and grime that occurs there in older pieces of furniture or other woodwork. Fig 6.6 shows the effect of a distressing wax on a pine-panelled surface.

MAKING DISTRESSING WAX

The best pigments for this job are raw umber, lamp black and a little burnt umber. You can use artists' powder colour or, better still, artists' oil colour.

1. Use the double boiler arrangement to melt some wax polish, as is shown in Fig 6.5 (see previous page).

2. Mix some raw umber with just enough white spirit or pure turpentine to liquefy it and then mix with the molten polish. Use sufficient pigment to make the polish quite dark.

3. Repeat the process with small amounts of lamp black and burnt umber. Keep the molten polish agitated and allow it to cool by taking the inner container out of the hot water.

4. The polish is ready to use when it has cooled and solidified again. Stir it regularly while cooling, to make sure the pigment stays in suspension.

USING THE WAX

Use it like normal wax polish, applying sparingly over the surface before rubbing into the edges and crevices of the work. You can also use it warm and molten on bare wood, following the warm-waxing method described earlier. This creates a very aged and distressed look and is ideal for 'ageing' new wood to blend in with old work.

OIL POLISHING

Our forebears not only used linseed oil as a furniture oil, but also other vegetable oils, such as poppy, walnut, olive and hazelnut. Now there are proprietary products available that offer a number of distinct advantages. These oil blends include teak oil, Danish oil and tung oil. They are specially formulated to be particularly easy to apply, become absorbed into the wood faster and dry more quickly. Before looking at the process of oiling, it is worth looking at what benefits oiling has to offer. The main advantages are that a fully oiled surface (if such a thing actually exists) is resistant to moisture and heat, making it a suitable finish for dining and coffee tables. Vegetable oils react slowly in the air, harden, and effectively form a protective skin. The formulation of proprietary furniture oils includes at least two ingredients other than oil: a solvent and a drier. The purpose of the drier is to speed up the reaction of the oil with the oxygen in the air – a process called oxidation – which in turn allows a shorter time between applications of oil. The solvent simply aids penetration of the oil into the wood.

A traditional recipe for a polish based on linseed oil is given in Chapter 16. Note that raw linseed oil is specified, and not boiled, which is more viscous and therefore slower to become absorbed by the wood, even though it does dry faster. However, any vegetable oil can be substituted for linseed, as the key feature of these oils is their property of hardening on exposure to air. Mineral oils are unsuitable, as they never harden.

APPLYING OIL POLISH

The first coat is best applied with a clean paintbrush. Don't flood the work, but be generous, without creating puddles. Leave for 24 hours and then rub vigorously with a lint-free cloth to remove surplus oil from the surface. Apply the second coat sparingly with a cloth and leave for another 24 hours before rubbing over again. At this stage, you may begin to see its sheen, but very absorbent wood will need quite a few applications before any real impression is made. The process of oiling can be made more effective by warming the oil first, using a double boiler. The heat makes it more fluid and aids absorption.

How many coats and how often? Oil polishing is never finished. There is always room for another coat. As a general rule of thumb, for new and stripped surfaces, I follow the regime of one coat a day for a week, followed by one coat a week for a month, followed by one coat a month forever. The surface will gain an unmistakable sheen and silky smoothness. The test is whether water runs off without penetrating the surface.

Sometimes heat or moisture will cause dulling, but this can be remedied with – yes – another coat or two of oil.

OILY AND WAXY RAGS – FIRE RISK

A WORD OF CAUTION!

Oily and waxy rags present an obvious fire risk if placed where there is a chance of contact with naked flames or incandescent objects, such as heating elements. What is perhaps less well known is the possibility of spontaneous combustion of cotton cloths used with linseed oil. In some circumstances, such as if a soiled rag is screwed up and kept in a warm environment, the rag can spontaneously combust. The terrifying consequences of this are obvious so it is important that you take the following precautions:

- Open up the rags and lay them out to dry outside and well away from combustible material. Once the oil has dried – an oxidation process with the air – the risk is reduced.

- Alternatively, and probably a better one, burn soiled rags so they cannot form a risk.

7 French Polishing

Acres of printed matter have been published on this method of finishing, yet it still retains a mystique and status that is rather baffling. It is the most hyped of the traditional finishes, and even with all the sophistication of modern finishing materials and methods, the skill of the traditional French polisher is highly prized and admired. To a large degree this can be put down to history: French polishing was introduced into this country during the first quarter of the nineteenth century, and the practitioners of the craft immediately kept the process a closely guarded secret.

The mechanics of the process are straightforward, but their application is notoriously difficult. At best, any written description can only convey the mechanics, although the odd tip here and there concerning working problems and the like will be useful. It is only through practising the techniques yourself that the skill can be acquired. Results may be disappointing at first, because there are so many variables that contribute towards a perfect finish that your first attempts may cause you some frustration. The effort is worth it once the skill is mastered. An important skill in French polishing is restraint in use. The temptation is to use it everywhere. A good French polisher is subtle, both with the polish itself and the associated use of colour.

French polish has some serious drawbacks. It will not resist heat, water, or alcohol, and even exposure to a damp, cold atmosphere over a period of time (i.e. during storage) may result in blooming. On the other hand, its smoothness, unique lustre and optical effects on colour and figure make it the most attractive of the hard finishes.

COMPOSITION OF FRENCH POLISH

French polish is a solution of shellac in alcohol. The concentration of the solution is called its 'cut', and for general French polishing a three- or four-pound cut is used. This means that three or four pounds (1.3–1.8kg) of shellac are dissolved in a gallon (4.5 litres) of alcohol.

There are several grades of shellac available, according to the degree of processing it undergoes before being made into polish. There is no real virtue in making your own French polish, as proprietary brands are of a consistent quality. The following descriptions are of the main grades of shellac and the polishes made from them:

- **GARNET**
  When dissolved in alcohol, garnet shellac forms a greenish-red brown polish that is ideal for use over dark or darkly stained woods. This is the darkest of the polishes, made from shellac flakes the colour of garnet stone.

- **BUTTON**
  The shellac produces a muddy brown colour, which is effective on old walnut which has faded to a honey-brown colour. However, it tends to give a rather unattractive colour-cast on brown or reddish timbers.

- **WHITE**
  Bleached shellac produces a creamy-white polish, which is useful as a general sealer and as a base for tinted polish. Used as a finish in its own right, it will produce a slightly grey colour cast, owing to the natural wax present in shellac.

- **TRANSPARENT (OR PALE)**

  If the wax is removed from white shellac, the resulting polish is a pale amber colour. It is ideal for use where the colour of the wood is very light or where that of inlays and marquetry must be preserved. If a dark polish is used, the natural colours in the wood are modified and much of the benefit derived by contrasting inlays will be lost.

'TABLE TOP' OR 'EXTERIOR' FRENCH POLISHES

Where a tougher finish is required while maintaining the familiar appearance of a French polished surface, there are the so-called 'table top' or 'exterior' French polishes. These are based on shellac in combination with other resins and are applied in the traditional way. However, they have a higher resistance to water, alcohol and heat so are ideal for tables and other high-wear pieces. They have their own special solvents. They are rarely used on external surfaces now because they are not as durable as more modern finishes, but can be used on the internal surfaces of window frames or internal doors that require the durability.

THE FRENCH POLISH RUBBER

The French polisher has a very simple, but important, tool for building up the familiar sheen – the 'rubber'. A rubber is a pad of upholsterers' cotton skin wadding over which is stretched a piece of clean, white, fine-grained cotton. How and when it is used will be described later.

MAKING THE 'RUBBER'

Figs 7.1 a–f show how a rubber should be folded to create a compact pear-shaped pad. The shape is important, especially the point, as this helps the rubber get into awkward and confined spaces on the work. The piece of skin wadding measures approximately 10in (25cm). It is folded in half as shown, and then into thirds before creating the point and folding into the pear shape.

MAKING UP THE WADDING CORE OF A FRENCH POLISH RUBBER

Fig 7.1 (a) Use upholsterers' skin wadding. The fine-textured, fibrous covering (the skin) sandwiches the cotton wool.

Fig 7.1 (b) Cut a piece roughly 25cm (10in) square.

Fig 7.1 (c) Fold in half.

Fig 7.1 (d) Divide the pad into three along the longest side, and fold into thirds.

Fig 7.1 (e) Form the point of the pad along the folded edge (the free edge is at the top of the picture).

Fig 7.1 (f) Form the pad into a pear shape, keeping the point.

FINISHING OFF THE RUBBER

Fig 7.2 (a) The point of the pad is directed towards one of the corners of the cloth.

Fig 7.2 (b) Fold the corner of the cloth over the point of the pad.

Fig 7.2 (c) Wrap the 'wings' of the cloth over the point and around it to secure the point.

Fig 7.2 (d) Twist the ends of the cloth to compress the pad and retain the pear shape. The twisted ends of the cloth should lie in the palm of the hand.

You can, of course vary the size of the rubber according to the job. As a general rule, if you measure the wadding with an outstretched hand, a hand span each way will produce a rubber that fits neatly into the palm of the hand.

Figs 7.2 (a)–(d), on the facing page, show how the rag, as it is called, is wrapped around the wadding. Note that the point of it is maintained. The method of holding the rubber is extremely important: the bottom needs to be in constant contact with the work, and an even flow of polish through the rag maintained. If held too high up, as in Fig 7.3 (a), the rubber will wobble and you will have little control, resulting in drag marks (called rubber burns) and loss of shape. Held as in Fig 7.3 (b), the face is pressed against the work, giving you greater control. It will also allow you to feel what is happening, for instance the early signs of drag, or the tell-tale scraping sensation of grit under the rubber.

A rubber has to be kept on the move at all times, to prevent it sticking. If, for any reason, you have to stop in mid-stroke, lift the rubber off the surface without stopping. Bad 'burns' or blemishes caused by the rubber sticking to the surface cannot be removed by continuing to polish over them; it only makes them worse. Stop, and allow the work to dry for half an hour or so before continuing, gently rubbing the blemish back with very fine nylon mesh abrasive.

Rubbers can be used over and over again if they are stored in airtight plastic or glass containers between periods of use, including between coats, even though the wait may only be a matter of minutes.

THE WORKING ENVIRONMENT

French polish is very sensitive to the environmental conditions during its application and for some time afterwards. Keep the temperature at about 20°C (70°F) for the whole polishing period (even between stages, when you are not actually polishing) and for a day or so afterwards while the work is hardening off. If the air is allowed to cool, the polish may 'bloom' as moisture condenses on the surface and becomes trapped in it.

HOW TO HOLD THE RUBBER

Fig 7.3 (a) Too high.

Fig 7.3 (b) Correct positioning of the hand and fingers to support the rubber and maintain good contact with the polished surface of the work.

The air needs to be free of excessive amounts of dust (no dusty jobs while polishing). In fact, it is advisable to have a separate room for polishing work, well away from major sources of dust.

After cutting back with abrasives between coats of polish, make sure that all dust is removed from the surface, using a tack rag. This is imperative to maintain a dust-free environment.

THE 'TACK RAG'

Rubbing down the work prior to polishing and between coats unavoidably creates dust. If you wipe the surface clear with a cloth, dust will be thrown up into the atmosphere only to settle onto the surface as you are polishing it, which is exactly what you do not want. Also, you may also leave specks of dust on the work.

Polishers use a 'tack rag' to remove dust from the surface of the work. This is simply a piece of open-weave cloth, such as stockinette, which has a slightly tacky surface to which dust adheres. They can be bought at any good decorating or polish supplier, but you can quite easily make your own:

1. Soak a piece of stockinette in water and wring out to leave it damp.

2. Now open out the cloth and sprinkle white spirit over it and work it through, wringing out any surplus.

3. Finally, sprinkle raw linseed oil over the cloth and work it through, but not too much oil as you want the cloth to feel damp to the touch, not sticky.

4. To use the cloth, lightly wipe it over the surface of the work after cutting back, without leaving a wet streak. If you look at the face of the cloth, you should see an accumulation of dust that has adhered to the damp, oily surface.

5. Store the cloth in an airtight container between uses, as this will keep it usable for weeks. You can always refresh the rag by repeating steps 1 to 3 when it begins to dry out.

SEQUENCE OF EVENTS

Wherever possible, take the work apart and treat each piece as a separate item. For example, take the doors off cupboards, remove drawers and separate the leaves in a table top.

If you want to stain the work, avoid using spirit-based dyes, as the solvent for stain and polish is the same (alcohol), and you run the risk of lifting the colour as you polish. Remember to follow the grain-raising procedure if you water-stain (see Chapter 5).

AFTER STAINING, THE SEQUENCE OF EVENTS IS AS FOLLOWS:

GRAINFILLING

Open-textured timbers will draw the polish straight into their fibres and the pores will remain open unless they are filled. It is difficult to achieve a mirror-gloss finish (the so-called piano finish) without first filling the grain. Grainfilling reduces the suction and provides a uniform surface upon which to build the substantial body of polish that is needed. If you want to keep an open-grained texture, leave out the grainfilling stage.

SKINNING IN

The initial stages of polishing are concerned with satisfying the wood's natural suction and in obtaining a smooth ground on which to apply successive layers of burnished French polish. You can use French polish for this, or a shellac-based 'sanding sealer'. The sealer is designed for this work and contains a fine powder that has two functions:

*   The powder is a bulking agent and has additional grain filling properties.

*   After the sealer has dried it is sanded smooth to form a flat, smooth ground for subsequent polishing. The powder provides 'bite' and aids sanding by helping the abrasive cut into the sealer.

Sanding sealer can be used as an alternative to grainfiller on close-grain timbers or where an open-grained texture is required.

COLOURING

Sometimes, after you have stained the work and you begun to polish it, you may find that the colour is not quite right. Either it does not match other areas of the work, or the whole piece has an unwanted colour cast, or is not quite dark enough. Colouring is the process where you remedy this by correcting the colour balance. Spirit-based dyes and pigments are used for this. Chapter 10 looks into this subject in more detail as it is a specialist area of finishing and the technique is appropriate for all finishes.

Some colour correction can be carried out immediately after staining if you are able to see a problem, and this is also discussed in Chapter 10.

BODYING

Many thin layers of polish are applied over the sealed surface using a rubber, until the desired depth of body and sheen is acquired. Some practitioners refer to the use of raw linseed oil as a lubricant for the face of the rubber, to prevent it sticking to the surface, but this can create more problems than it solves. The oil has to be taken off again and any residue may bleed through later, causing dullness. If you take care not to rush the work there is no need for oil. If the rubber appears to want to stick, simply stop and wait for ten minutes or so before continuing.

Bodying may take you several days, applying a 'body' of polish each day and allowing it to harden and shrink back overnight before applying another. Of course, this is time-consuming, but it is well worth the effort. Between bodies, the polish is given time to 'mature', i.e. it fully hardens and shrinks as the alcohol solvent evaporates. A surface that looks like a mirror after a body of polish has just been applied, may look less so the following day. This is especially the case with the first couple of coats.

SPIRITING OR STIFFING

This finishing process brings up the surface to a high gloss by burnishing it with the face of a rubber charged with French polish thinned with methylated spirits. Again, many practitioners advocate the use of

methylated spirits alone, but the risk of burning the surface, and so ruining all your good work, is quite high. True spiriting only uses methylated spirits, but the alternative use of thinned polish is just as good. As you become better and more confident, you can begin to increase the proportion of methylated spirits. Why it has the alternative name of 'stiffing' will become apparent when the process is described in detail.

BURNISHING OR DULLING

The high mirror-gloss associated with pianos is achieved by burnishing the hardened polish with a very fine abrasive a day or so after spiriting. In restoration work, it is often desirable to reduce the gloss because it looks out of place, especially when compared with original polished areas of the piece. Dulling is achieved with the judicious use of abrasives.

GRAINFILLING

Begin by partially sealing the wood with a brushed coat of thinned French polish in a ratio of three parts of polish to one of methylated spirits. Apply it quickly and thinly with a polishers' mop; avoid creating runs and ridges, as these are a real problem to remove later. Allow to dry overnight. This is not obligatory, but it does create a barrier that will make it easier to rub surplus grainfiller off the surface with less risk of clouding.

Proprietary ready-mixed grainfillers are available and should be applied according to the manufacturer's instructions, but you can make your own. Grainfilling is not recommended for all polishing situations because it causes problems by lodging in awkward angles. Small mouldings, turnings and carvings are filled with polish rather than grainfiller paste. This method will be described later.

MAKING THE GRAINFILLER

YOU WILL NEED:

- A strong, wide-necked mixing container and a spatula for mixing the ingredients.

- Whiting (this is available from polish suppliers or good art shops, as it is the main ingredient of gesso, which is used by artists to prime canvases and as a ground for gilding).

- Raw linseed oil (to act as a carrier for the filler).

- Artists' powder pigments – the earth colours such as umbers, siennas and ochres (again available from polish suppliers or art shops). These are used to colour the filler so that it does not show white in the grain. Match the colour of the pigment to that of the wood surface. For example, medium and dark oak-stained surfaces may need burnt umber; brown mahogany may need burnt umber with some burnt sienna; golden walnut may need yellow ochre or raw sienna, perhaps with a little raw umber; standard walnut may need raw umber with some burnt umber.

THE FILLER IS MADE UP AS FOLLOWS:

1. Place enough whiting in a wide container for the surface to be filled. It is better to make too much than too little and not be able to match up the colour in a new batch.

2. Mix enough powder pigment into the whiting to take off the extreme whiteness. You do not need a huge amount of colour. You may need to experiment with colours to find the exact match for the wood. The final colour of the filler, after it is mixed with oil, should be a little darker than the wood surface.

3. Mix the filler with enough raw linseed oil to form a paste the consistency of soft butter. It will be obvious at this point why you did not need a large amount of powder pigment. The oil will bring out the pigment's colour. If necessary, you can make adjustments to the colour by adding pigment, after first mixing it with a little white spirit to blend and help it work into the main body of the filler. Make sure it is all thoroughly and uniformly mixed.

APPLYING GRAINFILLER

The application method is the same for proprietary or home-made fillers. Proprietary filler is usually in the form of a stiff paste that will need thinning down a little to make it the consistency of soft butter. A stiff paste will be too difficult to apply and force into the grain.

Use the solvent recommended on the container.

Home-made filler should be at the right consistency, but if you find it too difficult to apply, you can thin that with a little white spirit; not too much – otherwise it will be too thin and runny to be any use.

The following steps describe how to apply the filler:

1. Take a piece of open-weave hessian and fold it into a pad that fits snugly in the palm of the hand, as you will need to keep a comfortable grip on it.

2. Dip the face of the hessian pad into the filler and pick up enough to cover the face.

3. Rub the filler hard into the surface of the wood, using a small circular motion and forcing filler into the pores. Tackle a small area and make sure the pores are adequately filled. Prevent a large accumulation of filler on the surface by rubbing the filler outwards over the surface. There should just be a thin film over the work (see Fig 7.4a). The filler on the surface will start to stiffen as the wood begins to absorb the oil, so keep it moving over the work.

4. Once the filler has been 'worked out' and you can no longer force it into the pores, refold the pad to present a clean surface and rub the surplus filler off the surface across the grain (this will also help to force filler into the pores). Do not leave any obvious accumulation, there should only be a thin oily smear left (see Fig 7.4b).

5. Repeat the process over another small adjacent area.

6. Continue working like this until the entire surface has been treated.

7. Finally, take a clean pad of hessian and wipe the surface clean of obvious signs of filler. Leave overnight to allow the oil to sink into the wood and dry.

APPLYING THE GRAINFILLER

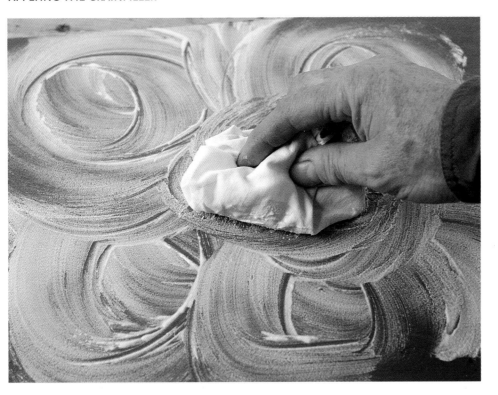

Fig 7.4 (a) Rub the filler paste into the pores of the wood using a circular motion and firm pressure.

Fig 7.4 (b) Rubbing off surplus filler across the grain.

SKINNING IN

USING FRENCH POLISH

If you used grainfiller, give the work a good rub-over with a clean lint-free cloth to remove residue. Make up a rubber and charge it with polish by taking out the pad of wadding and dipping its face into polish poured into a wide-necked container (see Fig 7.5a). Remove surplus polish by stroking the face of the wadding against the side of the container (see Fig 7.5b) before replacing the rag over the wadding.

Apply a fairly generous amount of polish to the surface with the rubber, i.e. enough to satisfy the wood's suction, but not so generous that you create puddles or ridges of polish, which are exceptionally difficult to remove once they have dried in. The purpose of this phase is to 'prime' the wood by creating an even film over it. The aim is not to create a mirror gloss, simply a flat film that acts as a stable foundation on which to build the polishing coats.

You will apply the polish in stages, and may need to wait a while between coats. If you do, store the rubber in an airtight container so it does not dry out. Look after this rubber, because you will use it for the bodying and finishing stages. In fact, 'skinning in' is a good way to break in a new rubber.

Recharge the rubber with polish as it dries out and you have to apply excessive pressure. If the rubber tries to stick to the surface, glide it off and wait five to ten minutes before continuing. It is important to prevent the rubber sticking as it will tear the coat of polish, creating a scar than can be difficult to remove. If you use any abrasives between coats, use a tack rag to remove the dust.

STRAIGHT STROKES

Using light pressure at first, apply the polish to the work in straight, slightly overlapping strokes. There should be an obvious full-width streak, but no ridges of polish which would be difficult to eliminate later. If there are several pieces to be polished (remember you may have dismantled the furniture to make it easier to polish), work them in rotation, covering each piece once (see Fig 7.6 on the facing page). If you are working on a single piece, leave it a couple of minutes before moving to the next stage.

CHARGING THE RUBBER WITH POLISH

Fig 7.5 (a) Dip the face of the pad into the polish to draw it into the wadding.

Fig 7.5 (b) Squeeze out surplus against the side of the container.

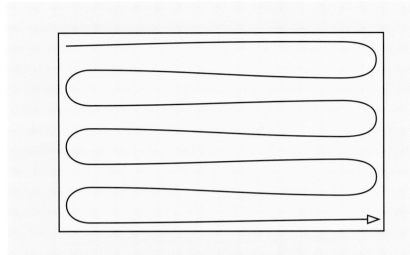

Fig 7.6 Applying the first sealing layer in straight strokes along the grain.

LARGE FIGURES OF EIGHT

Apply a second coat in large figures of eight (see Fig 7.7). This helps to force the polish into the grain, while making it easier to move the rubber across the surface. Again, work all pieces in turn. This cycle ensures that no piece is ever forgotten.

STRAIGHT STROKES

Finally, apply a coat using straight strokes along the grain. Do not overlap them, as this will be asking for trouble (i.e. sticking). Glide the rubber onto one end and off the other (see Fig 7.8 overleaf). If you are working on a single surface, rather than working through a cycle of several parts, the surface may resist the movement of the rubber, which will tend to stick. You can do one of two things: slow down, apply less pressure and gently glide the rubber over the surface; or stop and wait a few minutes for the film to dry off a little before continuing.

Allow the work to rest for 10–15 minutes, then examine it and, if there are any specks of dust, gently rub them off with fine nylon-mesh abrasive. Also look to see if the film of polish is even across the whole surface. If there is an even sheen without areas where the polish has obviously been drawn down into the wood, resulting in a 'dry' look, you can stop. Also, if you have used grainfiller, make sure that there is no open grain.

If neither of these conditions is met, you need to apply another coat using the same straight, figures of eight and straight routine. Most jobs will only need two or three coats done in this way, with a 15 minute or so resting period between each of them. When you have

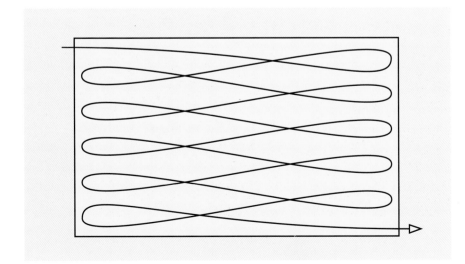

Fig 7.7 Forcing the polish into the grain using a figure of eight movement

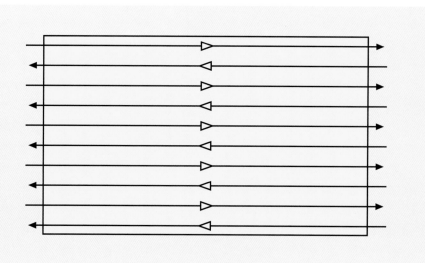

Fig 7.8 Finishing off the first coat with straight strokes along the grain, gliding the rubber on and off the edges.

finished, store the rubber in its container ready for the next stage, then leave the work to harden overnight.

FINAL PREPARATIONS

The surface you have created will not be perfect; there may be rubber burns or dull streaks caused by friction. This is not important, so long as there has been no pooling of the polish or ridges produced. So long as it is flat and generally smooth. When you examine the surface the next day, the look will be different. It may be less shiny, and it will certainly have shrunk back. This is normal and is why you must leave plenty of time between the stages. Before continuing to the next stage (colouring or bodying), you must gently cut back the film of polish with fine nylon-mesh abrasive to create a 'key' and to remove any specks of dust.

USING SANDING SEALER

This should be brushed onto the work with a soft-bristled brush, along the grain and well brushed into it. This is quite tricky, as you must prevent ridges and puddles which are difficult to remove when they dry in. Do not overcharge the brush, and work quickly as shellac sealer dries very quickly. Leave the work for a couple of hours to harden before inspecting it, then smooth it with 320 grit abrasive paper, removing the dust with a tack rag.

After gently sanding, the surface should be flat and smooth (and the grain full, if this is required). Take care not to cut through to the surface of the wood, and create a light area where stain has been removed. If you do, you will have to touch up the area with stain allow to dry and apply sealer over the area.

Some of the more absorbent and open-grained woods may require a second coat of sanding sealer, which should also be smoothed after a couple of hours. Leave overnight to harden properly.

COLOUR CORRECTION

At this point, you will know what the final colour will be like. Colouring is described in detail in Chapter 10, so it is sufficient at this stage to simply say now is the point where colouring occurs.

BODYING

If you have stored the rubber properly, it should be in a good enough condition to use for 'bodying'. At the same time, it will have been broken in, and its shape established, and the wadding primed as a responsive reservoir of polish.

Test for the quantity of polish by pressing the face of the rubber against a sheet of white paper. Fig 7.9 a–c show the result of having the right amount, too little or too much. If too much, open up the wadding and allow it to dry out for a while before retesting. If necessary, recharge with polish. Fig 7.10 shows how a rubber should be charged, by opening up the wadding and pouring in a small quantity from a bottle.

Overcharging will cause ridges, through flooding of the surface, that cannot be removed easily, and an

**TESTING FOR THE QUANTITY OF POLISH
IN THE RUBBER DURING BODYING**

Fig 7.9 (a) Not enough polish: the face of the rubber is quite dry.

Fig 7.9 (b) Too much polish: the surplus will be forced out of the face of the rubber, causing ridges or pooling on the surface.

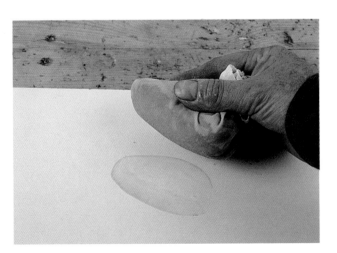

Fig 7.9 (c) The correct amount: a definite 'footprint' with the polish able to flow in a controlled way out of the rubber.

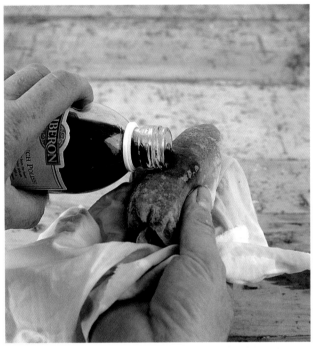

Fig 7.10 Charging the rubber with polish for bodying.

excessive flow to the surface will cause the rubber to stick or 'burn' previous layers of shellac. Press the face of the rubber against white paper as a test, as in Fig 7.9, and squeeze out any surplus, distributing the remainder throughout the wadding. Body the work using the method described below. Again, if several pieces or sections are being polished, follow the sequence of coating each piece in turn.

Figure 7.3(b), on page 57, illustrates how the rubber is held. Mastering the movement of the rubber is not easy, as the natural way is to use the wrist. In fact, you need to keep the wrist firm and activate the rubber's movement from the elbow and shoulder.

APPLYING A 'BODY' COAT

SMALL FIGURES OF EIGHT

The centre of the work is bodied with small figures of eight along the length of the grain (see Fig 7.11 overleaf). Cover the central portion and then work around the edge, to ensure that the whole piece is covered. The path of the rubber should be obvious, but under no circumstances must there be very wet tidemarks. Stop if the rubber is clearly too wet, and allow the surface to dry for an hour or so before gently cutting back again with fine nylon mesh abrasive.

LARGE FIGURES OF EIGHT

Next, work large overlapping figures of eight along the grain, over the whole surface (see Fig 7.7, on page 63). It may be necessary to divide the surface into two or even three areas if it is very long (see Fig 7.12, facing page).

By this stage you should be experiencing some resistance to the motion of the rubber. The best way to describe the amount of pull is to carry out a simple experiment. Simulate the movement of the rubber by rubbing the ball of your hand over the surface of a clean window pane. The pull you feel is pretty much what you need to have during bodying. Apply only enough pressure on the rubber to see the polish being deposited and to achieve the pull just described. Any excessive pressure will cause tearing up, but some friction is needed to pull the polish flat as it is laid on the surface.

As the rubber begins to dry out, you will need to increase pressure slightly and then recharge with polish if its face feels dry when tested against the back of your hand. If it feels cold and moist, there will probably be enough polish to continue, but if you are experiencing problems, such as excessive drag or even no drag at all,

because very little polish is flowing through, then change the rag, as it is probably clogged. Also, change the rag if you can see tiny scratch marks or hear the sound of grit under the rubber; you will also be able to detect the presence of grit by the feel of the rubber. Experience will tune your sense of touch to the different responses of the rubber. As resistance increases your inclination will be to speed up the movement of the rubber – do the opposite. Slow down, hold the rubber firmly and keep it gliding at a regular pace over the surface. If it starts to judder, as it tries to stick, glide the rubber off the work and leave it for few minutes before continuing. Juddering may also be a sign that there is not enough polish in the rubber.

STRAIGHTS

Finally, to eliminate the path marks of the figures of eight, work along the grain with slightly overlapping straight strokes; each stroke should glide on and off the edges (Fig 7.8 on page 64). It may be necessary to repeat once or twice if any swirls still remain, in which case take extra care with the pressure you apply, as the risk of sticking is increased. It may be better to recharge the rubber and use light pressure. Experience will again tell you which is better in different circumstances.

When all the pieces to be polished have received a full body as outlined above, allow about 15 minutes or

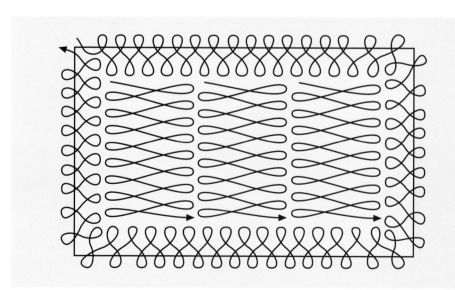

Fig 7.11 Apply the first body coat in small figures of eight.

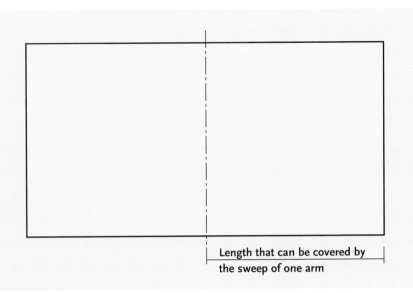

Fig 7.12 Long surfaces (e.g. dining tables) can be tackled in sections.

Length that can be covered by the sweep of one arm

so for it to dry before applying another coat in the same sequence. From now on, the pull on the rubber will increase, so you will need to take care to prevent tearing up the softened polish. There is always the temptation to move the rubber at some speed, but this is a mistake. The rubber movement should always be deliberate, well controlled, and at a slow enough speed to achieve the result without sticking. Any faster, and you will almost certainly tear up the film of polish.

I am frequently asked how many coats should be used, which is a difficult question to answer, as this depends upon a number of factors. Basically, continue bodying until you gain a good, deep sheen, or until the rubber is determined to stick to the work. At this point, leave to dry and harden overnight, during which time the film of polish will shrink a little.

The following day, if you want a deeper body, cut back with 400 or 600 grit silicon carbide (wet-or-dry) paper, or a piece of very fine nylon pad abrasive, to remove surface blemishes such as rubber marks or adhering dust, before bodying up again. Remove the dust with a tack rag. Three or four bodies applied in this way over several days will be enough for most purposes, but for a mirror finish you could need more. You have to judge the situation for yourself.

Immediately after each body, there may be minor rubber marks; do not worry about them at this stage as they should disappear as the polish hardens. It is important to allow overnight drying because the polish film shrinks as it hardens and takes on a different appearance so you can only make a judgement then.

STIFFING OR SPIRITING

In most cases this will be the final stage, which is designed to burnish the polish to a high gloss. Use French polish thinned down a little with methylated spirits in a ratio of three parts of polish to one part of methylated spirits.

After leaving the polished work to harden overnight, cut back the film very slightly with a very fine nylon mesh abrasive or 600 grit wet-or-dry paper. Charge the stiffing rubber with the thinned polish and, using very light pressure, as though applying another body, apply the polish in straight, very slightly overlapping strokes along the length of the grain (as in Fig 7.13 overleaf). The stroke must be very straight or you will produce an arcing pattern to the finish. When all the pieces have been treated in this way, wait a few minutes and then repeat the sequence. This time you should start to feel a very definite pull (hence the term 'stiffing') as the surface film is partially dissolved and pulled flat by the rubber. The resistance to the rubber's movement may tempt you to speed up, but that is a mistake as the surface will be 'burned'. The trick is to slow down the movement and pull the rubber firmly and evenly over the surface. As always, adopt the rule that if you experience difficulty, stop, wait for a time then start again.

Stop when you have achieved a high, even gloss. There may well be some minor blemishes, such as minor dullish rubber marks. These usually disappear as the surface hardens. If not, repeat the stiffing process after a few hours.

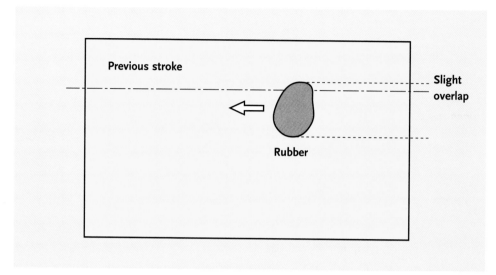

Fig 7.13 Straight, and slightly overlapping strokes in stiffing.

OTHER FINISHING METHODS

For most purposes stiffing produces a really good finish, but there are other ways, each of which is done after stiffing.

BURNISHING

This will produce the classic mirror finish often associated with pianos. A very deep body of polish is needed to make it effective, and grain-filler must be used to give a full grain. If you attempt to burnish an open-grained finish, the burnishing cream will collect in the pores and turn them white.

After stiffing, allow the work to harden for at least a day in a warm environment. Special burnishing creams are available from polish suppliers. Pour a little of the cream on to a damp, soft polishing cloth and quickly distribute it evenly over the whole surface, without applying any pressure. Burnish the surface, using straight strokes along the grain and only a little even pressure. As the cream begins to dry, stop and wait for it to dry fully before wiping off along the grain with a soft, dry polishing cloth. It may be necessary to repeat the burnishing process if it has not reached the full mirror gloss. Any residual haze caused by excess wax can be removed using a reviver (see Chapter 13 for information on how to use a reviver, and Chapter 16 for recipes).

DULLING

The high gloss left by stiffing may be too much, as may be experienced in restoration work, and must be dulled

down. The easiest way to do this is with a very fine nylon mesh abrasive pad or 0000 steel wool (which is also very fine) lubricated with wax polish to reduce its cutting action.

Dip the nylon mesh abrasive, or pad of steel wool, into clear wax polish and rub it over the work in full-length strokes along the grain. Apply gentle even pressure to ever so slightly cut back the high gloss (see Fig 7.14). After working over the entire surface, wait for the wax polish to dry before buffing. Inspect the surface and make a judgement about it. If it is still too glossy, repeat the process.

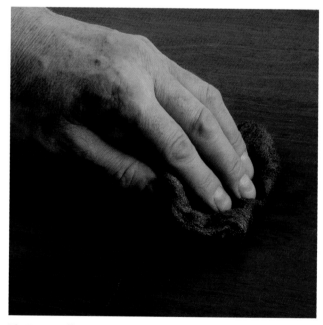

Fig 7.14 Dulling with wire wool, or nylon mesh abrasive, lubricated with wax polish. Rub gently along the grain direction.

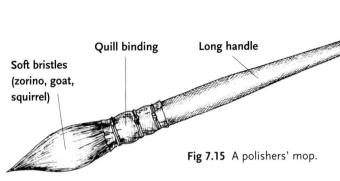

Soft bristles
(zorino, goat,
squirrel)

Quill binding

Long handle

Fig 7.15 A polishers' mop.

The effect you are trying to create is that of a satin finish which resembles many years of hand-waxing seen on old furniture. That is why this technique is very common in furniture restoration: nothing gives away the fact that restoration has taken place more than a newly French-polished surface. The dulling process removes the 'new' look of the finish.

POLISHING AWKWARD AREAS

This chapter has so far explained how to polish straightforward flat surface. Many items will have awkward areas that are inaccessible to a rubber, such as carvings, intricate or small mouldings, and corners. This is where the polishers' mop and squirrel pencil brushes come in. A mop is a very soft-haired brush, with goat or squirrel hair, or a combination of hair called zorino – this latter being the most useful kind – quill-bound to the handle (see Fig 7.15).

CARVINGS AND MOULDINGS

Use the mop to apply polish in two or three coats (to replace skinning in and bodying). The first coat can be with a sanding sealer to kill any tendency to absorb subsequent coats of polish. Apply thin coats, as runs and drips must be avoided. On carvings, work the polish well into the crevices and undercuts. Mouldings can be burnished or dulled using the methods described above after a day or so.

CORNERS, TURNED WORK AND QUIRKS

Even a well-made fad or rubber cannot reach right into all the angles (quirks), which will appear dry. Use a squirrel pencil brush to apply polish into these areas (see Fig 7.16).

POLISHING FAULTS

There are several things that can go wrong.

BLOOM

The polish will go dull and milky during application in an environment which is cold and damp, or if a draught is blowing directly over the surface. Cut back after allowing time to harden, adjust the working environment and recommence polishing if the problem is not too great. However, if the surface is badly bloomed, you may have to strip it and start again.

RUBBER BURNS

Caused by too much pressure or too wet a rubber. The symptoms are dull streaks and, in bad cases, a degree of roughness. Allow the work to harden, cut back and polish again. Very faint rubber marks often disappear as the polish hardens.

FINGERPRINTING

If the work is handled too soon after polishing, it may show the impressions of fingers and hands, even though it appears hard. If this happens, again, allow it to harden, cut back and repolish.

Fig 7.16 Using a pencil brush to apply polish in awkward areas a rubber cannot reach.

8 Varnishes

We classify a 'varnish' as any solution of a gum or resin in a solvent which dries to produce a hard and transparent finish. Early varnishes seem to have derived from the use of oil as a polish. Considerable secrecy surrounded the manufacture and application of these varnishes, but it has been established that many craftsmen were using finishes that were manufactured by dissolving natural resins such as copal in linseed oil (and even alcohol in some cases). This was certainly not an easy process, as the oil had to be heated to encourage the resins to dissolve, which naturally gave rise to some dangerous practices. It is only in the last few centuries that alcohol-based varnishes became known – French polish is an example of a spirit varnish. Today, it is not practical to make your own varnishes. Even specialist needs, such as violin and guitar making, are met by a number of suppliers.

Traditional varnishes based on natural resins were not colourless. Their colour ranged from pale amber to dark brown, depending on the resins used. The development of a colourless varnish did not occur until the twentieth century, when the chemical industry discovered the ability to produce synthetic resins with impressive mechanical properties. More recently, environmental and health and safety legislation has prompted the industry to produce environmentally and user-friendly materials (see Chapter 3).

A classic example of this is the development of durable water-based products in response to the desire for a 'safe', solvent-free formulation. From a consumer's point of view, they are a dream – easy to apply, minimal odour (therefore no respiratory irritant factor), fast drying and, perhaps the greatest convenience, the ability to clean brushes in water and detergent, so no rows of dry, ruined brushes in gummed-up jam jars.

TYPES OF VARNISH

The descriptions given here are confined to modern varnishes that are readily available over the counter.

ALKYD RESINS

These synthetic resins are the basis of the external varnishes frequently referred to as 'yacht' or 'marine'. They are heavy-bodied varnishes and require longer drying periods. If brushed on too thickly, they easily 'sag' (i.e. wrinkle), and take days to dry. They are relatively flexible, and so will move with the wood to some degree. They are also more resistant to corrosive chemical attack, hence their use in marine environments.

'Marine' varnish has excellent flow and gloss properties, readily settling into a smooth film from the brush and drying to a high gloss that aids water repulsion.

POLYURETHANE

Heralded during the 1960s as a significant breakthrough in paint and varnish technology, this polymer was marketed on the basis of its extreme hardness and durability. In fact, these very properties are also its source of weakness – brittleness. Polyurethane is not particularly elastic and, if subjected to conditions in which the expansion and contraction of the object is taking place routinely, then the varnish film will ultimately crack and flake away. Other problem areas are window boards, which are subject to condensation running onto them from the glass; and to strong sunlight, or, more specifically, the sun's heat, as the extreme fluctuations in moisture levels within the wood, and the expansion and contraction due to the temperature changes, will cause rapid breakdown of the varnish film.

However, it should be remembered that there are few finishing materials that can tolerate such adverse conditions over a long period, and polyurethane represents one of the most effective interior varnishing materials where durability and toughness is required.

WATER-BASED VARNISHES

These products are rather different in nature in that they are not solutions of resin, which is the conventional definition of a varnish, but are emulsions. Resins that have the properties required of an effective varnish are not soluble in water. If they were, they would have a very limited value. By emulsifying the resins in water the need for powerful organic solvents is eliminated, resulting in a product that is effectively odourless and volatile-vapour-free. Consequently, they are both safer for the environment and your health, than solvent-based products.

Since water-based products dry very quickly, compared with traditional varnish drying times, the convenience factor alone makes them a good investment. If a varnish can claim to be re-coatable within two hours, it is possible to complete a three-coat varnishing job within a single day.

The varnish also looks different in the can. Open a tin of clear polyurethane varnish, for example, and peer into a transparent, pale amber liquid. Open a can of varnish, and you are presented with a thick, opaque, milky-white liquid. This can be somewhat alarming if you are not expecting it, but it does dry clear. The appearance is due to the emulsification which effectively creates a cream.

A wide range of products are available both for interior and exterior use; once the water has evaporated, the resin film is what gives the varnish its properties.

MICROPOROUS

These varnishes are described as 'moisture vapour permeable' (MVP). Their claim to superiority is the ability to tolerate what, to others, is normally an unacceptable level of moisture in the wood, providing it is not actually wet. Moisture trapped in wood will gradually evaporate and try to escape. All other types of varnish will eventually crack and peel as a result of this, but MVPs actually allow the vapour to escape through the varnish film – provided it is not too thick – but at the same time provide a barrier against water penetration. In effect, the varnish allows the wood to 'breathe' by providing what you could describe as microscopic pores (see Fig 8.1, on the facing page). If at the same time you combine this property with preservatives and ultraviolet filtering pigments, you have the basis for an extremely useful exterior grade varnish. MVP products, if properly applied, will generally last longer than alkyd varnishes.

It is pointless putting an MVP over an existing non-MVP varnish, even if it is sound, because the original coat will obviously not allow vapour to pass through. If you intend to use an MVP, you must strip off all traces of any other finish.

MVPs may be solvent-based, but the latest generation of exterior varnishes is water-based and they are also ideal for high humidity areas internally, such as kitchens and bathrooms.

COLOURS AND FINISHES

Varnishes may be clear (uncoloured) or pigmented (stain varnishes). They may have a matt, satin (eggshell) or gloss finish. It is beyond the scope of this book to describe individual products, as there are so many and the choice available can cause confusion, but the principle to adopt when selecting a product is to consider:

- Where the product will be used

- What environmental conditions need to be tolerated

- The decorative and protective functions of the finish

- Your preference for solvent- or water-based products

MVP VARNISH

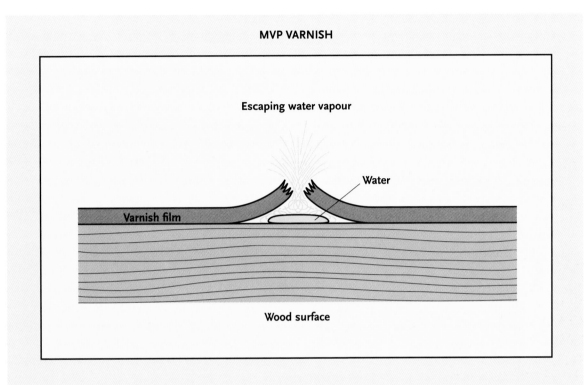

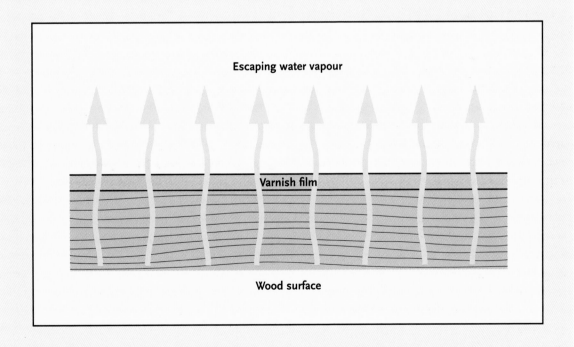

Fig 8.1 Top: Non-MVP varnish blisters and peels as water vapour tries to escape.
Bottom: MVP varnishes allow the vapour to escape through the varnish film.

You can then match these requirements to the products lining suppliers' shelves.

Varnish stains have several advantages over using a stain followed by a clear varnish. First, you are saving time; second, because they are heavy-bodied, they do not become absorbed too deeply into the wood. This makes them ideal for wood of a variable absorbency, which would lead to patchy staining. Varnish stains will produce a more even colour. The main problem with them, however, is that they cloud the surface, especially the darker colours. The figure in the wood becomes obscured if you use more than a couple of coats because of the pigments.

VARNISH BRUSHES

It is important to reserve a set of brushes solely for varnishing. On no account should those already used for paint be used, as the varnish will be contaminated with specks of paint. As in most things, the best results

Fig 8.3 Storing a varnish brush by wrapping the bristles in stiff paper to preserve their shape.

are more easily obtained by using the best tools. Traditional varnish brushes are oval in cross section, which allows the bristles to 'flow' around edges and mouldings (see Fig 8.2). They can, of course, be used for paint as well, but they are more expensive than normal paintbrushes.

Remember, cheap brushes always drop their bristles in the varnish film. If you have spent a lot of money on a brush, you will want to keep it in good condition. When you have finished varnishing, clean it several times in white spirit and then in a proprietary brush cleaner before rinsing it out in cold water. Warm soapy water is all that is needed for cleaning brushes used with a water-based varnish. If you are not intending to use the brush in the near future, wrap the bristles in brown paper as shown in Fig 8.3. This retains the shape of the bristles.

There is no need to clean the brush between coats, as the bristles become more pliable and softer with use, producing a better finish. The bristles must be kept wet

Fig 8.2 Traditional varnish brushes have an oval cross section.

Fig 8.4 Keeper varnish – note the bristle tips do not touch the bottom of the container.

with varnish, and you will need a glass container and keeper varnish. Keeper varnish is thinned varnish in which the bristles of the brush are suspended without touching the bottom of the jar, so they do not become bent. Fig 8.4 shows a keeper jar. Note the cover which prevents dust settling and the nail through a hole in the handle to keep the bristles clear of the bottom. The varnish is thinned in the ratio of three parts varnish to one part of white spirit (or water if for water-based varnishes). A clean, lint-free rag is used to remove surplus varnish prior to re-coating.

SURFACE PREPARATION

Previously varnished surfaces that are sound, i.e. not peeling, may be re-coated without stripping, but must first be washed down with water and mild detergent, allowed to dry and then 'keyed' by being rubbed down with fine abrasive paper and the dust cleaned away with a tack rag. If the finish is cracked or peeling, it will have to be stripped. If you intend to use an MVP varnish and the old finish is not MVP, then it must be stripped, even if it is sound.

If the work is being stained, water stains will provide no problems of compatibility, but there may be a problem with oil stains. These are based on the same powerful solvent as solvent-based varnishes, and there is a risk of lifting the stain when brushing on the first coat of varnish. This can result in patchiness, especially if you have not allowed a long drying period for the stain. Allow plenty of drying time for the stain and do not become too vigorous in brushing on the first coat of varnish, and it should not create a problem.

Water-based varnishes are compatible with all types of stains.

APPLYING THE VARNISH

Whatever type of varnish you are using, the basic rules are all the same. Absolute cleanliness of tools and surfaces, a strict adherence to drying times recommended by the manufacturer, and several thin coats rather than one thick.

NEW, PREVIOUSLY UNFINISHED OR STRIPPED SURFACES

These will be rather absorbent, so thin the first coat with 10% white spirit (water in the case of water-based varnish) by volume. Apply fairly generously, avoiding runs. Remove any bristles that find their way on to the work as soon as you notice them, and never allow them to dry in.

When thoroughly dry, 'de-nib' (remove dust specks) with 240 grit abrasive paper, taking care not to cut through to the wood, and tack rag the surface clean

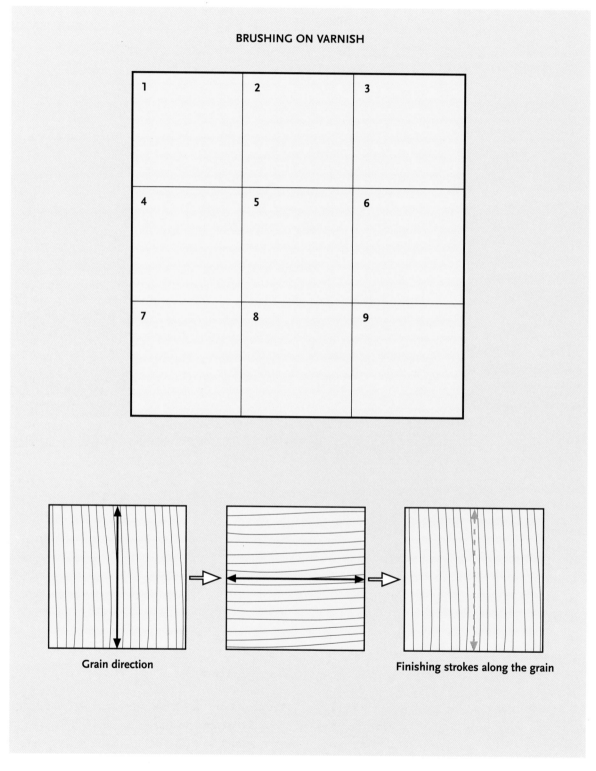

Fig 8.5. Top: Varnishing large flat areas by sectioning off into manageable sections.
Bottom: Sequence of brushstrokes to create a good finish and ensure full coverage.

of dust. Subsequent coats should be applied undiluted and each cut back with 600 grit wet-or-dry, using water and a little washing-up liquid as a lubricant. Dry and then tack rag before applying the next coat. The final coat is not cut back unless you are burnishing or dulling (see overleaf).

The number of coats depends upon the circumstances. In general, the more wear or the more adverse the conditions are, the more coats will be needed. The exception to this is MVP varnish, where no more than two are applied, or the microporosity becomes diminished. Furniture should receive two or three coats, floors at least four (more in heavy traffic areas). If yacht varnish is used on external woodwork, apply four thin coats. If you intend to burnish the varnish to a high gloss, apply one extra coat (not applicable to MVP).

OLD, SOUND VARNISHED SURFACES

Wash these down with water and a little washing-up liquid, and allow to dry. Provide a key by rubbing down well with 240 grit paper, and tack rag clean of dust. The work is now ready to receive two coats of varnish, with a rub down between coats using a fine abrasive. When recoating MVP varnish, use only one coat to preserve the porosity, or better still strip it and start afresh.

BRUSHING TECHNIQUE

Brushing technique goes a long way towards producing a good finish. Narrow-sectioned timber such as legs and rails, has the varnish brushed on along the grain, while larger areas, such as table tops, panels and floors, require a different technique to ensure every portion is covered. The brush is charged with varnish to two-thirds of the bristle length, and the tips squeezed against the side of the container. Large areas are varnished in sections, each capable of being covered by, say, two or three brush-loads. The varnish is first brushed out along the grain, then across it. Finally, the bristle tips are drawn very lightly along the grain in straight strokes to eliminate any brushstrokes – the so-called 'laying off' strokes.

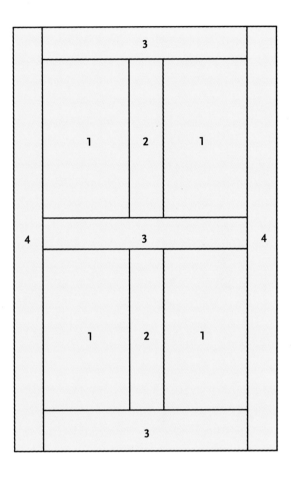

Fig 8.6 Sequence in varnishing components of panelled work.

Move on to the next section, and repeat until all the surface is covered. Each section should overlap very slightly so that there are no 'dry' areas. Fig 8.5, on the facing page, illustrates this approach, and Fig 8.6 shows the order of varnishing panelled work. The direction of the finishing strokes should always correspond to the grain direction.

ALTERNATIVE FINISHES

Varnished surfaces can be burnished to a mirror gloss or dulled to semi- or full matt, though it is easier to use satin or matt varnishes for this. In all cases the varnish should be allowed to harden for as long as possible, at least 48 hours for polyurethane, and up to a week for yacht varnish.

BURNISHING

The surface must be free of all blemishes such as dust specks and brush marks, and must be perfectly flat. To prepare for burnishing, the varnish film needs to be cut back with 600 grit wet-or-dry with water and detergent, until all blemishes are removed and there are no bright, glossy areas. Wipe, allow to dry and then tack rag. You can buy special burnishing creams, but 'T-Cut' or a similar abrasive fluid will do the job.

Slightly dampen a pad of mutton cloth large enough to fit into the palm of your hand, and spread burnishing cream over its face. Distribute the cream over the surface without any pressure, then apply pressure in straight lines along the grain. Do not linger in any one area as this can result in cutting through the film, or even melting it because of the heat generated through friction. Clean off the cream with a clean cloth, allow to dry and then buff along the grain. A haze may remain, but this can be removed with a polish reviver (see Chapter 16).

Open-grained surfaces should not be burnished, as the cream will accumulate in the pores, leaving an unsightly white deposit which is difficult to remove. If necessary, apply more coats of varnish to achieve a full-grain finish.

DULLING

A gloss varnish can be dulled down to a full matt by gently rubbing along the grain with 0000 wire wool or fine nylon mesh abrasive. On the other hand, you may still want a sheen, but may dislike the 'plastic' high gloss that a varnish can sometimes give. In this case lubricate the abrasive with some wax polish and then buff the surface when the wax has dried, after an hour or so. You can vary the degree of dulling by varying the amount of time you spend abrading the surface.

THE VARNISHING ENVIRONMENT

It is not always possible to operate in ideal conditions, especially with exterior work, and you can expect to have to compromise to some extent. However, the best conditions for varnishing are:

- A warm dry atmosphere to aid drying, avoiding direct sunlight. For exterior work, this limits the times to spring and summer. Begin and finish work as early as possible, to allow maximum drying time before the chill of the night arrives (which also increases damp).

- A dust-free atmosphere. Although this is all but impossible, reduce any disturbance of already settled dust. This means not moving anything (if at all possible), and certainly means no woodwork in the workshop at the same time as varnishing. Constant use of the tack rag before varnishing surfaces is important — you can't always see the dust until the varnish is applied. If there is a dust-lifting breeze, don't varnish.

VARNISHING FAULTS

Most varnishing problems arise because of poor environmental conditions, inadequate preparation or careless application. The commonly occurring faults are:

NIBS

These are dust particles which have become trapped in the varnish film. To some degree they are unavoidable because of the drying times of solvent-based varnishes, but they can be reduced. Adequate sanding between coats prevents the cumulative effect of particles being added to each successive coat. This, and careful dusting down with a tack rag, are essential practices. The working environment may be difficult to control, but be sensible. Nibs are most disfiguring on gloss finishes, as they are very obvious, so you have to take meticulous care.

TACKINESS

If a varnish film is still tacky after the recommended drying time, the following may be the causes:

- Cold or damp working environments will inhibit the evaporation of solvent from the film. The remaining 'solid' component of the varnish will not harden either.

- Heavy coating, especially with heavy-bodied varnishes such as yacht varnish. The problem here is that the film of varnish 'skins' over. The surface dries trapping wet varnish beneath it, and the solvent can now only escape very slowly, resulting in an extension of the drying time. Be particularly careful with yacht varnish, where it is better to apply several thin coats rather than one heavy.

- Old varnish may have deteriorated to a point where it will not dry properly because certain active ingredients responsible for speeding up the drying may have evaporated. If you must use an old tin of varnish that has been knocking around in the cold, damp garage, then add a dash of paint drier (such as terebene), just in case. Better still, dispose of it.

BLOOM

Varnish applied to damp wood or in damp conditions may develop a milky, opalescent surface, caused by moisture trapped in the varnish as the solvent evaporates. In mild cases, a thorough sanding before revarnishing should eliminate it, but in more serious cases there is no alternative to stripping and revarnishing, after the wood has been allowed to dry or environmental conditions improve. It does not always occur straight away, and may develop some months after the varnish was applied. Whenever it occurs, damp is the culprit. If you suspect this possibility, use a microporous varnish.

SAGGING

A fault found mostly on vertical or sloping surfaces, resulting from loss of adhesion between coats of varnish. Runs and drips occur almost immediately the varnish is applied, but sagging may happen long after the varnish has apparently dried. Loss of adhesion will result from one of two causes, often the combined effect of both (see Fig 8.7).

Bad surface preparation will prevent a good bond between coats, especially if there is grease or dirt present. Combine this with an excessively thick coat of varnish applied over it, and you have the perfect conditions for sagging. The top coat may 'hold', and even apparently dry, but gravity may have other ideas. The weight of the film may be greater than the adhesive force holding it to the previous layer.

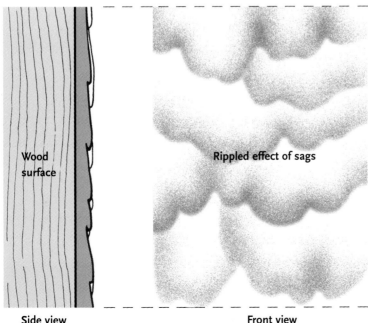

Side view   **Front view**   **Fig 8.7** Varnish 'sag'.

Wood surface

Rippled effect of sags

VARNISHING FLOORS

The main properties of a varnish formulated for floors are extreme durability, toughness and short drying times, to allow recoating within as short a time as possible. A rapid drying time also reduces the amount of dust fallout from the air that becomes trapped, which is especially important if you want a high gloss.

Some specially formulated floor varnishes are based on relatively fast-drying solvents and polymers, with the associated need for adequate ventilation. One or two require an extended period when the floor cannot be used, to allow time for the varnish to harden or cure by chemical action. Clearly, these will produce very tough finishes, but may be rather inconvenient. At the other end of the scale, there are water-based floor varnishes that are very fast-drying and allow you to re-coat within a couple of hours. In theory, you could finish a varnishing job within the day, making this type ideal for areas that are in constant use.

You may have to compromise, though, if you need to keep a traffic lane open. If that is the case, varnish the rest, and come back to the traffic lane once the rest has hardened sufficiently to use, but this may produce problems in colour matching if you are staining.

The greatest embarrassment comes when you trap yourself in a room surrounded by wet varnished floor, which does happen! Always plan your varnishing so that you start at the point furthest away from the entrance/exit and finish at the point where you can escape. Always close off the room afterwards, to prevent roaming animals and humans ruining your good work (see Fig 8.8.). As for ventilation, you will need a little, but do not leave windows wide open, otherwise you will invite dust, leaves and other windblown material to take up permanent residence. And of course the neighbour's cat may leave a pawmark or two as documentary evidence of its visit.

Heat in the room will aid drying, but do not overheat, as the varnish will go tacky while you are

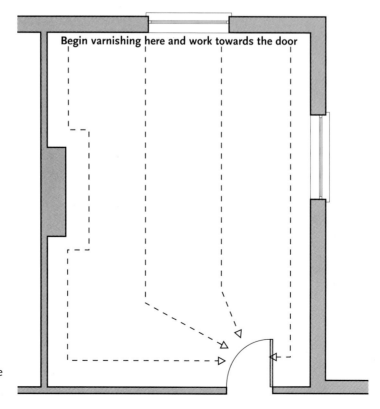

Begin varnishing here and work towards the door

Fig 8.8 Make sure you do not varnish yourself into the corner of a room.

applying it. Warmth also increases the vapour levels if using a solvent-based product. As for the number of coats, this depends to some extent on the manufacturer's recommendation, but high-traffic areas will need at least four or five coats. If you have the time and patience, it is a good idea to gently hand sand between coats.

WOOD STRIP AND PARQUET FLOORS

After laying a wood strip (not artificial laminate) or parquet floor, some time must elapse to allow the adhesive to dry and its solvent to evaporate. A couple of days should be enough. Instructions for laying these floors include the procedure for cleaning off adhesive from the surface. Always brush the floor prior to varnishing. The first coat of varnish can be thinned up to 10% with the appropriate solvent, i.e. white spirit or water, depending on the type of varnish used. Subsequent coats are applied unthinned.

FLOORBOARDS

If possible, fill the gaps between old floorboards with wedges of wood, as the gaps are a source of draughts and small objects and liquids may fall between them. Fig 8.9 shows how to do this. The wedges should be left proud until the glue has dried and then planed flush. The boards can be sanded and stained afterwards, if required.

MAINTENANCE

Maintaining a varnished floor is not difficult, although dressing with wax is not recommended. Nothing more than damp dusting will be needed, unless it is heavily soiled. As soon as any wear begins to show, wash the floor, sand it lightly to create a key, and put on a couple of coats of varnish. If it is allowed to deteriorate too much, you may have no option but to strip and begin the process of varnishing all over again. So it pays to attack wear as it becomes noticeable.

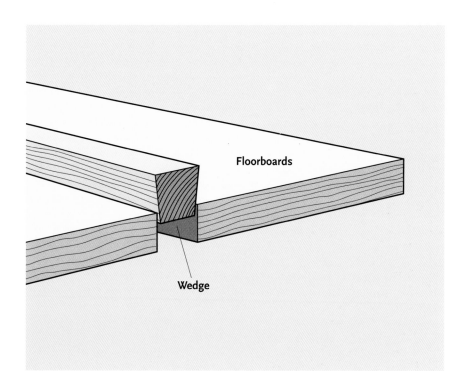

Floorboards

Wedge

Fig 8.9 Wedging gaps between floorboards – the wedges are planed flush when the glue has dried.

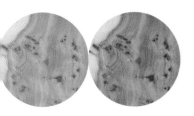

Spray Lacquers

Traditional finishes do not easily lend themselves to the rigours of modern mass-production methods, as they are all relatively labour-intensive, or are simply not durable enough. If stains and polishes can be sprayed, then time is reduced and turnover increased. The puzzling thing is that modern methods and materials are often considered inferior to traditional methods and materials. There is a widely held view that the 'modern' does not have the 'tradition' of craftsmanship. In short, if you spray it on the wood, the 'human' element must have been removed. The truth is that the application of a modern synthetic lacquer requires great skill and technical knowledge. As for the materials themselves, there is a great deal to commend them.

Modern synthetic spray lacquers were developed in response to the demands of the furniture industry, which wants its furniture to look good when it is sold and to remain that way for a long time. At the same time, it has to to be quick to produce.

TYPES OF LACQUER

The early lacquers were relatively crude materials. Today, the market demands higher specifications for wood finishes, and highly sophisticated formulations have been developed.

It is possible to categorize all furniture finishing lacquers into one of the following groups:

- Nitrocellulose (N/C) lacquers
- Pre-catalyzed (P/C) lacquers
- Acid-catalyzed (A/C) lacquers

- Water-based lacquers

The decision about which lacquer to use should be based on a number of considerations, the main ones being:

- Ease and economy of application.
- Consistent quality and reproducibility.
- Utility.
- Product range (of colours and finishes, i.e. gloss, semi-matt, matt).
- Environmental and health and safety considerations.

Lacquer manufacturers produce detailed data sheets on each of their products covering composition, conditions of use (including health and safety and environmental factors), and instructions on how to prepare and apply the product. When buying lacquers you should always ask for this information as the data sheets also provide information about related products, such as grainfillers, stains, thinners and compatibility with other products.

NITROCELLULOSE (N/C)

Cellulose is a naturally occurring plant material, and N/C was originally derived from this, but is now entirely a product of the petrochemical industry. Historically, it is the earliest of the modern synthetic lacquers, and its survival today is the result of its value as a basic finishing material. Cellulose synthetic lacquers are relatively cheap, very fast drying, and can be hand finished to produce a high-quality surface, using a process called 'pullover', which involves the skilful use of solvents quite reminiscent of French polishing. Pullover will be described in more detail later.

They are useful general purpose lacquers but, because they are not resistant to heat, moisture, or strong solvents, their use on commercially produced furniture is now quite limited.

PRE-CATALYSED (P/C)

Most wood finishes harden in a very simple way, by solvent evaporation. The majority of wood finishes are solutions of a solid in a solvent and as the solvent evaporates the solid component is left behind as the hard film. By the very nature of the process, if a polish hardens by evaporation of solvent, it can be softened again by the same solvent. In other words, they are reversible. The property is useful as it can be used to strip the finish, but it does mean that the finish is susceptible to intentional damage. There are many occasions where a tougher, irreversible finish is needed.

Pre-catalysed lacquers work by drying initially, through solvent evaporation, and then by 'curing', i.e. hardening by a chemical reaction called 'polymerization'. During manufacture, a catalyst is added to the lacquer. This is a chemical agent that accelerates polymerization. While the lacquer remains in its container the catalyst is not active, but as soon as it forms a thin film over the substrate and is in contact with the air, the chemical process begins. Over a period of several hours after initial drying, the lacquer film undergoes the chemical change. The resulting lacquer film is made of a different, tougher chemical than the original.

During the initial stages, pullover can be used to burnish the polish to a high gloss, but after a short period it will not work, because polymerization has begun to change the nature of the chemical.

Pre-catalysed lacquers have rather better mechanical properties of resistance to moisture, many solvents and, to some degree, heat and scuffing. Pre-catalysed lacquers usually present some resistance to strippers, and it is often necessary to make several attempts before they work.

ACID-CATALYSED (A/C)

This is also a material that hardens by chemical reaction brought about by a catalyst. In this case,

though, the lacquer and catalyst are not mixed at the manufacturing stage, as the lacquer has a short pot-life once the catalyst is added. These lacquers are called 'two-pack' products, for obvious reasons.

Before use, the catalyst is added to the unthinned lacquer and mixed well, prior to thinning for the spray gun. The ratio of catalyst to lacquer is crucial, and the instructions provided in the manufacturers' product data sheets concerning mixing ratios must be adhered to. This is usually in the ratio of one part catalyst to ten of lacquer. The speed of curing and the ultimate performance of the lacquer will depend upon it.

It takes a few days for the polish to cure completely, but then it provides a very tough finish that will resist heat, water and solvents. It is widely used in the furniture industry, as it is not only good for the customer who wants an easy-care surface, but it is also ideal for the manufacturer who needs to store and transport the products to arrive in pristine condition.

WATER-BASED LACQUERS

The problem with the lacquers described so far is that they are based on powerful and volatile organic solvents. They pose a potential risk to the environment and the health and safety of the user. The industrial use of these products requires manufacturers to install sophisticated equipment that filters overspray out of the working area, and extracts harmful materials from the air. The Environmental Protection Act 1990, the regulations it has spawned, and the various international agreements and EU legislation on environmental controls have encouraged manufacturers and users to consider cleaner technologies and better waste management. Water-based lacquers are an example of how the industry has responded.

While the overspray (i.e. the cloud of lacquer that forms a mist in the air) is still a hazard because of its particulate nature, the solvent is not, because it is water. The air can be drawn away and the lacquer particles filtered out. There is no need for concern over the water vapour component that finds its way out of the system (see Spray Booths, page 85).

THINNING AND FILTERING LACQUERS

THINNING

Lacquers are sold in a slightly concentrated form and may need to be thinned prior to use. Individual equipment, environments and lacquers will vary, so stick to the recommendations provided in the technical data sheets.

Manufacturers' technical data provides information on thinning, including which solvents to use, thinning rates and optimum lacquer 'viscosity'. The higher the viscosity, the thicker the liquid. The viscosity of a lacquer is determined using a viscosity cup (a Ford No. 4 cup – see Fig 9.1), which has a known volume and an accurately sized aperture at the bottom. It is filled with the lacquer, which is then allowed to drain from the aperture. The time taken for the cup to drain as a continuous stream is a measure of the viscosity. Timing of the flow stops when the stream begins to break up. Manufacturers specify the viscosity required for spraying by referring to this time. For example, a lacquer may be specified as requiring a viscosity of 50–60 seconds, in which case it needs to be thinned so that it flows continuously from the viscosity cup for between 50 and 60 seconds.

In damp weather, solvent-based lacquers may be thinned with 'anti-bloom' thinners. These have a slightly retarded evaporation rate to reduce the risk of bloom. Water-based lacquers will, of course, be thinned with water.

FILTERING

The aperture in the spray gun nozzle is very small, so any grit in the lacquer will cause spitting

Fig 9.1 A Ford cup used to measure lacquer viscosity.

Fig 9.2 A spray booth.

and an interruption to the flow. This will ruin the work. Filtering the lacquer as you pour it into the spray gun reservoir will prevent this. You need to use special disposable cone filters that have a fine mesh at the bottom, and these are available from the lacquer supplier. Use a new filter for each job you do – they cannot be re-used.

SPRAY BOOTHS

All the materials so far described in this chapter, with the exception of water-based lacquers, contain and are thinned with powerful solvents, which are hazardous to health if the operator is not adequately protected and the environment if not contained. They also represent a fire or explosion risk. Suffice it to say that extreme care must be exercised in the use of these materials, and always follow the recommendations provided on the product data sheets.

The flammability of these products is measured by flash point, which is the temperature at which a vapour and air mixture will ignite. (Refer to Chapter 3 for more information.)

Spray booths reduce this risk by containing the overspray and evaporating solvent within a confined space. The overspray mist is drawn out of the booth by a fan and through a filter and recycling system that removes particulate matter and solvent vapour. Spray booths range in sophistication from simple portable cubicles for the small workshop to large enclosures for factories. They are an essential part of the kit for spray work, to protect you and the environment.

CONVENTIONAL SPRAY EQUIPMENT

Spray equipment delivers lacquer to the work with some force as a mist of fine droplets, a process called atomization. If everything goes well, the droplets adhere to the substrate, fuse together and flow into a full and even film. The nozzle, or air cap of the spray gun is responsible for atomizing the lacquer by forcing it through a narrow aperture. The basic principle is that a jet of compressed air is mixed with the stream of lacquer, causing it to atomize.

SPRAY GUNS

Fig 9.3 shows the basic anatomy of a gun. The air and lacquer become mixed at the cap (nozzle), but there are three ways in which the lacquer may be delivered to the nozzle: suction, gravity feed, or by pressure.

- **SUCTION** The lacquer is held in a container (called a cup) attached beneath the gun. Air escaping at the cap creates a vacuum immediately in front of it, which siphons the lacquer from the cup. These guns are referred to as siphon fed (see Fig 9.4).

- **GRAVITY FEED** The cup is attached above the body of the gun, allowing gravity to assist the flow of lacquer to the cap. This arrangement allows for a high degree of fine-tuning of the spray pattern, which makes the tool ideal for small touching-up jobs and for special effects (shading, speckling, etc.), as well as being a good general-purpose gun (see Fig 9.5, on facing page).

Fig 9.3 Spray gun anatomy.

Fig 9.4 Suction or siphon-fed gun.

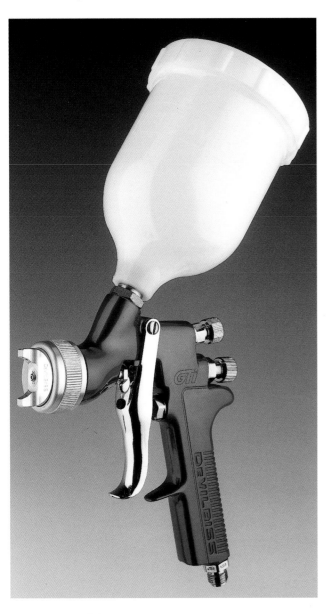

Fig 9.5 Gravity-fed gun.

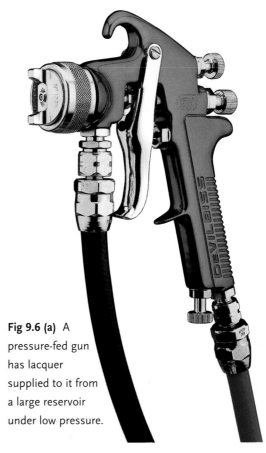

Fig 9.6 (a) A pressure-fed gun has lacquer supplied to it from a large reservoir under low pressure.

- **PRESSURE FEED** For production runs, a high volume of lacquer will need to be fed to the gun. The material is held in a container some distance away from the gun and supplied to it under pressure provided by air, which is fed separately into the container. Apart from the fact that you do not need to constantly refill a low-capacity cup, this system of lacquer delivery is ideal for heavier-bodied lacquers. Suction and gravity-fed systems will usually require lacquers to be thinned with appropriate solvents, but this is often unnecessary with pressure-fed guns, so each pass of the gun over the substrate deposits a heavier film of lacquer. Fig 9.6 (a) shows a pressure-fed gun, where the lacquer is delivered to it via a pressure hose, while Fig 9.6 (b) (overleaf) illustrates the components of a pressure-fed system.

ATOMIZATION

The business end of a spray gun is called the air cap. This directs compressed air into the stream of lacquer to atomize it. Its own performance is affected greatly by the fluid tip and needle as they meter and direct the lacquer into the air stream. Together, the cap, needle and tip are called a 'nozzle combination'. It is possible to fit different nozzles to the gun to suit a range of circumstances, and manufacturers' catalogues often contain tables to help you select the most appropriate nozzle. The choice depends upon:

- What is available for your model of gun.

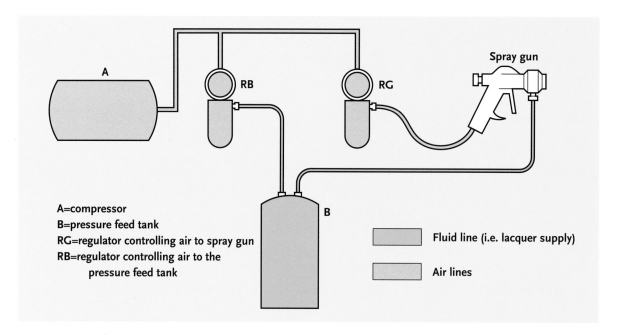

Fig 9.6 (b) The components of a pressure-feed spray system.

- The type and viscosity (thickness) of the lacquer.

- The rate at which air is supplied to the gun from the compressor, in cubic feet per minute (cfm) or litres per minute (l/min), and the air pressure, measured in pounds per square inch (psi) or bars.

INTERNAL MIX NOZZLE

Where low air volume and pressures are involved, the gun is usually designed to mix the air and lacquer inside the cap before expelling them. These guns are typical of those supplied with DIY kits. They are not designed for extended periods of use.

EXTERNAL MIX NOZZLE

The lacquer passes through the aperture of the cap, and is then atomized by jets of compressed air directed into it outside the cap (see Fig 9.7). This type of gun is designed more for professional use, and will produce high-quality finishes. These guns have higher air consumption and pressures, and need higher-capacity air compressors. Fig 9.8 shows the anatomy of internal and external mix caps.

Fig 9.7 Small DIY external mix gun.

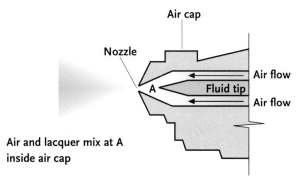

Air cap

Nozzle

Air flow

A   Fluid tip

Air flow

Air and lacquer mix at A
inside air cap

Fig 9.8 (a) Internal mix cap.

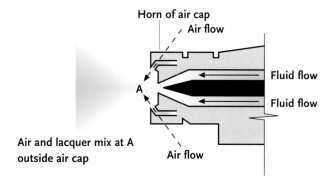

Horn of air cap

Air flow

Fluid flow

A

Fluid flow

Air and lacquer mix at A
outside air cap

Air flow

Fig 9.8 (b) External mix cap.

COMPRESSORS

As with spray guns, the choice of compressor is a matter of horses for courses. A compressor may be rated according to the power of the motor or, more usefully, by the rate at which it can supply air, e.g. 8cfm at 50psi.

Another important point to consider is whether the compressor has an air receiver and if so, its volume (i.e. a tank which will store the compressed air at high pressure). The small DIY units frequently do not have a receiver, so air is supplied to the gun directly from the compressor unit. The value of the receiver is that it ensures the gun has a constant supply of air, without fluctuations in pressure or volume flow.

Fig 9.9 shows a compressor unit suitable for use with a single gun. It is vital to match the gun to the compressor, as the latter must be capable of supplying air at the rate required by the gun's nozzle. It is pointless running a gun whose nozzle requires 10cfm at 50psi, if the compressor can only supply 6cfm at 50psi, as the gun will simply run out of air. As a general rule, the compressor should be rated higher than the air consumption required by the gun.

AIR REGULATOR/FILTER

It is essential that the pressure of the air in the receiver is reduced before delivery to the gun. It must also be clear of any contaminants, as these would be carried onto the substrate with the atomized lacquer. The main contaminants are water vapour, oil from the motor, and dust.

In the portable compressor shown below in Fig 9.9, a pressure switch operates when the pressure in the receiver reaches 150psi. The air to the gun passes through a pressure regulator and filter which reduces the pressure to that required by the gun, and the filter removes all the contaminants at the same time.

Fig 9.9 Portable compressor unit for low volume work.

Note that there are also two gauges: one reads the reservoir pressure, the other the line pressure, the pressure of the air delivered to the gun. This latter pressure can be adjusted to suit the particular requirements of the job.

HVLP SYSTEMS

The problem with conventional spray systems (which have been around since the 1920s) is that they are wasteful. Very fine atomization, and hence the ease with which a good finish can be achieved, comes at a price – very high levels of wastage. A very high proportion of the material simply finds its way into the air as a mist! High volume low pressure (HVLP) systems have been developed as one response to reducing waste and environmental impact.

The system works in a similar way to conventional spray systems except the guns are designed to deliver an atomized spray of fluid using an air pressure of 10psi or less. Since the lacquer is being ejected with less force, less finds itself dispersed in an overspray. The disadvantage is that some operators find the guns do not create as fine a finish, and so more hand finishing is needed.

AIRLESS SYSTEMS

In airless systems, atomization is achieved by pumping the lacquer to the gun nozzle under high pressure and forcing it through the nozzle, so that it breaks up into the atomized mist. Fig 9.10 (a), above, illustrates a small DIY unit, and Fig 9.10 (b), on the facing page, shows a professional airless unit.

Like HVLP systems, there is less wastage through overspray. However, the finish from an airless spray system may not be as good as that from a conventional air system.

SPRAYING TECHNIQUE

You need to understand the operation of the spray gun. There are two controls, one for the rate of flow

Fig 9.10 (a) Small DIY airless kit.

of lacquer to the nozzle, the other to control the distribution of the lacquer as it leaves the gun, ranging from a pencil spray to a flat, wide fan. The air pressure is controlled at the compressor. In general, the wider the fan, the more lacquer you will need to flow to the nozzle to maintain a good spray pattern. The trick is to coordinate pressure, fan and material flow so that just the right amount of lacquer reaches the wood to give a good, full coat, which doesn't run. Virtually all the problems associated with learning the technique revolve around this. The thing to do is to set the pressure at the recommended level and fiddle around with flow and fan to create the ideal spray pattern, as shown in Fig 9.11. Before spraying any lacquer on your work, practise on scrap wood first to get the pattern right.

The spraying distance should be 8–10in (20–25cm) from the surface, and keep this as constant as possible. Always keep the gun moving while lacquer is leaving the gun, and keep it parallel to the work as any arcing will produce an uneven coat. Work along the grain (this also helps as a reference), and make each pass of the gun overlap the last by 50% (see Fig 9.12, on page 92). This will ensure that there is a full, even coat.

Good trigger action is important. As you depress the trigger, the air is turned on first, and as you depress further, the lacquer flow to the nozzle is activated. It is critically important that you begin a pass by allowing

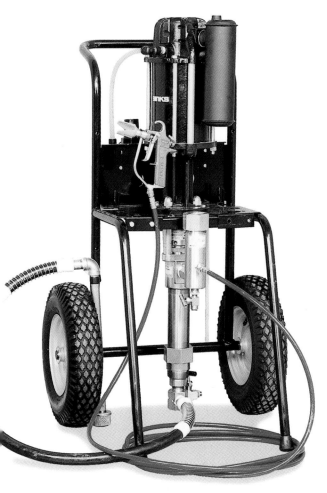

Fig 9.10 (b) Professional-quality airless system.

the air to flow first, then release the lacquer into the nozzle. Each pass should start before the gun reaches the surface, and end after it has passed the other side (see Fig 9.13, overleaf). This will prevent sudden heavy deposits as the gun is switched on, or dry areas as it is turned off.

WORKING PROCEDURE

The working environment is important: the air should be warm and dry – above 20°C (70°F) – to aid drying and prevent blooming. Your heat source must not have a naked flame or incandescent element. In small workshops, oil-filled electric radiators are good.

SURFACE PREPARATION

Initial preparation of the substrate is the same as for any other finish. Chapter 4 outlines the procedures in some detail, but should imperfections require filling with stopping, special cellulose-based stopping should be used and this will be available from your polish supplier.

STAIN

There is also an important compatibility issue here. Water, NGR or non-strike stains are the only acceptable stains to use. Traditional oil and nitrostains will bleed into any cellulose lacquer, and may cause cissing (see page 93) with water-based lacquers.

Non-strike stain is designed to be sprayed onto the work as it is very fast drying, and brushing or wiping the stain on may lead to tidemarks. Spray the stain

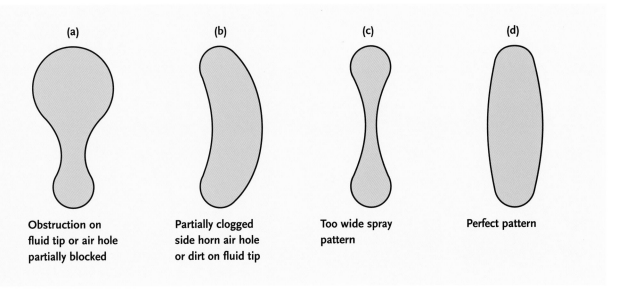

(a)	(b)	(c)	(d)
Obstruction on fluid tip or air hole partially blocked	Partially clogged side horn air hole or dirt on fluid tip	Too wide spray pattern	Perfect pattern

Fig 9.11 Finding the ideal spray pattern.

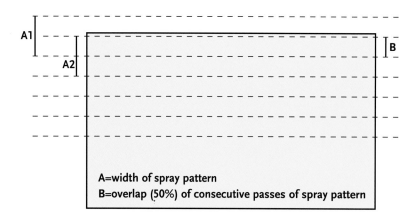

A=width of spray pattern
B=overlap (50%) of consecutive passes of spray pattern

Fig 9.12 Overlap each pass of the gun by 50%.

onto the wood as a full wet coat, and if necessary even out the colour with a cloth. A non-strike stain can usually be sprayed with lacquer within the hour.

GRAIN FILLING

Special cream grainfillers are available for use under the different lacquers. Refer to the lacquer product data sheet for details. They are applied in the same way as described in Chapter 7 on French polishing. Rub it into grain in a circular motion, wiping off surplus across the grain. Work small, manageable areas at a time.

TONING

Chapter 10 looks in detail at the general theory and practice of correcting colour errors, but mention needs to be made at this point of the procedure of colour correction in spraying. Sometimes the colour after staining is not quite right, and a correction needs to be made. This is done by spraying toning lacquer over the stained surface, or even after a sealing coat of lacquer. You can buy toning lacquer in a range of colours, or make up your own by tinting the lacquer you are using with non-strike or NGR stains. This whole process of colouring is highly skilful, and relies on the polisher's colour judgement.

SANDING SEALER

The work is now sprayed with a coat of sanding sealer. This stage is equivalent to fadding in French polishing, where the aim is to seal the wood, to reduce its suction and provide a smooth base coat for the top coats. You should buy a sanding sealer compatible with the finishing lacquer, i.e. pre-catalysed sealer for P/C and A/C lacquers, and cellulose sealer for N/C lacquers.

FINISHING COATS

Two coats will usually be sufficient and allow at least an hour between them. Gently de-nib after the first coat and dust off with a tack rag. For matt and satin lacquers, the job is now complete and the work should be set aside to harden for a few days (especially in the case of catalysed lacquers).

PULLOVER – FOR A MIRROR GLOSS

Special solvents called 'pullover' when applied with a rubber (like French polish), gently soften the surface and 'pull' it flat. Use figure-of-eight strokes, as in French polishing, followed by straight strokes along the grain. The final finish should resemble a good French-polished surface. Pullover cannot be used on water-based lacquers.

It should be borne in mind that this process is really only effective on N/C lacquers, because the solvents will soften the lacquer surface. A/C and P/C lacquers harden by chemical reaction, and so will not

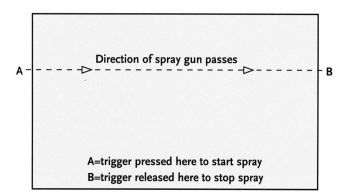

Direction of spray gun passes

A=trigger pressed here to start spray
B=trigger released here to stop spray

Fig 9.13 Trigger action to ensure even application of lacquer.

pullover readily, although reasonably good results can be obtained on P/Cs, provided pullover takes place within about two hours of the final application. Pullover can be applied to N/Cs at any time after the final coat has dried.

BURNISHING – FOR A MIRROR GLOSS

This should only be carried out on full-grained finishes, as any open grain will trap the burnishing cream and show up as unsightly white flecks.

The lacquer must first be cut back slightly to remove any blemishes, such as the odd speck of dust, using very fine (400–600 grit) wet-or-dry paper used wet, before being wiped clean, allowed to dry, and then dusted down with a tack rag.

A burnishing cream contains very mildly abrasive powders and is applied over the whole surface in straight strokes along the grain with damp mutton cloth. Continue rubbing over the surface along the grain until the surface has polished to a high gloss. Allow the cream to dry on the surface before buffing along the grain with a dry cloth. The surface may look slightly hazy, but this can be removed using a reviver.

Burnishing should only be carried out on lacquers that have been allowed to harden for at least a couple of days. All types of lacquer can be burnished, but in the cases of P/C and A/C products, where pullover is not all that successful, it is the only effective way to achieve a mirror finish.

LACQUER DEFECTS

There are a number of possible defects that can occur when spray lacquering. The following are the most common:

CISSING

This manifests itself as pockmarks, and is caused by water or oil entering the lacquer spray. The source is the compressor itself, and cissing indicates a filter that is either faulty or in need of cleaning. The filter should be drained after each spraying session. The only cure for cissing is stripping and starting again.

ORANGE PEEL

The name aptly describes the effect, where the surface has the texture of orange peel. This is caused by poor atomization of lacquer, perhaps because it is too viscous, the air pressure is too low, or the application of too heavy a coat. The surface can be rubbed down before respraying, but there is often still residual orange peel, and it is better to attempt pullover. Failing that, strip and respray.

BLOOMING

If the surface develops a milky-white appearance, moisture has become trapped in the lacquer film. The causes are a cold, damp atmosphere where, as the solvent evaporates, the surface cools down to below the dew point of water, and air moisture condenses out on to the wet lacquer. It may burnish out if mild, but otherwise strip and respray.

GRANULAR TEXTURE

A very common result for the inexperienced sprayer, caused by either having the gun too far away from the surface or by using too fast a pass. Either way, insufficient lacquer is put onto the wood to produce a full film. When you run your hand over it, the surface feels like fine abrasive paper. Rub down and respray.

TACKINESS

A thick film of lacquer may skin over, trapping wet lacquer beneath and preventing the solvent from evaporating. It can take two or three days for the film to dry. The only thing you can do is wait and keep the atmosphere warm.

SPITTING

This is a problem within the gun, where grit, oil or water has managed to enter the mechanism, interrupting the airflow. The remedy is to clean out the gun and, if necessary, disassemble the compressor filter and clean it with cellulose thinners, to remove excess oil. In any case, the filter should be drained after each job and cleaned with cellulose thinners periodically.

10 Colour Correction

One of the most difficult areas of woodfinishing is colour. Occasionally a stained surface appears to be the right colour until you start polishing. The change in colour can sometimes be quite striking, and there are two basic reasons for this. First, the polish itself may be coloured, and will modify that of the wood. The other main cause of colour change is the way light is reflected from the surface. Polish changes the reflective properties of the surface and this results in a colour change.

In Chapter 5, a reason for staining work was to create a uniform colour, but in restoration work this purpose often needs to be modified. When a repaired surface is re-stained, it tends to result in uniformity, but this may not be consistent with the rest of the piece, where age and wear has resulted in much greater variation. In these circumstances, it is necessary to use additional colouring techniques to recreate the look of age.

On the other hand, you may simply have made a mistake. For instance, mahogany stains are often rather red. When used on mahogany itself, this redness becomes quite fiery and may need toning down. This illustrates the need for testing the colour on scrap wood before applying it to the work itself, but even that is not an infallible approach.

Another common reason for 'colouring' is to paint out a blemish, such as a small scorch mark, or to disguise small areas of repair. This process is called 'painting out' and a detailed description of this is given on page 101.

PRINCIPLES OF COLOUR THEORY AND CORRECTION

To correct a colour cast you need to have a good and thorough understanding of how light and colour behave. For example, it is only by knowing how colours interact with each other that using a 'wash' of green stain or polish to correct a fiery red cast becomes the obvious solution.

THE COLOUR SPECTRUM AND COLOUR VISION

The colours of the rainbow were taught to us all at school, with prisms and rays of light passing through them. To practice colour correction, you need to understand the behaviour of light and colour. Fig 10.1, overleaf, shows the colour spectrum and how the colours are represented conventionally, from red through to violet. The order helps us to understand how our eyes and brains perceive colours when dyes and pigments are mixed.

Fig 10.2 (a) represents a blue-painted object. When light falls upon it, some is reflected and the rest is absorbed by the object. The material reflects its own colour, i.e. blue, and absorbs all the other colours, except for a small amount of the two colours that are adjacent to blue in the spectrum – green and indigo – but we are barely aware of them. By the same argument, a yellow-painted object will reflect yellow light and absorb all the others, except for a little green and orange, see Fig 10.2(b). The clever bit is when we mix the blue and yellow paints together. Why do we see green?

Fig 10.1 The colour spectrum.

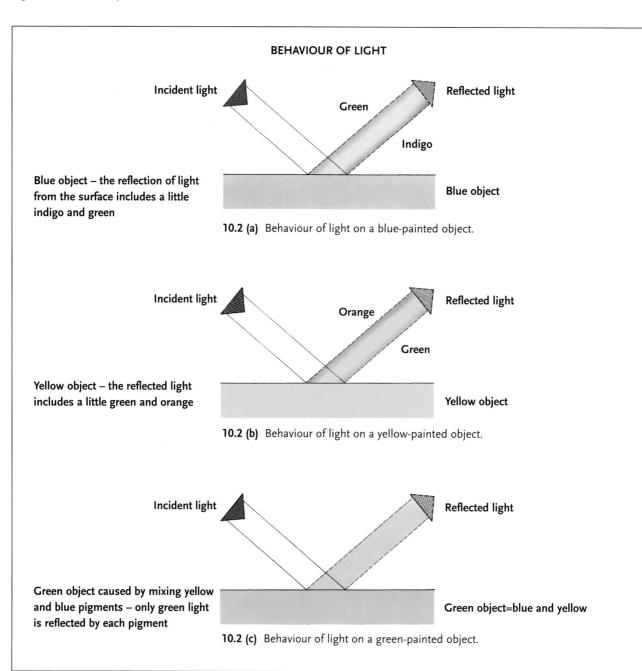

Fig 10.2 The behaviour of light: **(a)** A blue-painted object **(b)** A yellow-painted object **(c)** A green-painted object.

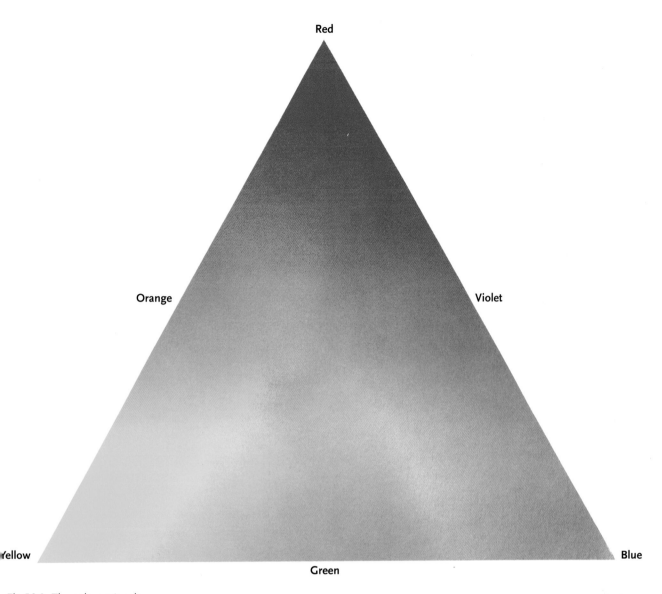

Fig 10.3 The colour triangle.

When light strikes the green object, the blue pigment will attempt to reflect its band of colours (blue, with a little indigo and green), but the yellow pigment will absorb the blue and indigo and attempt to reflect its colour band (yellow, with a little green and orange). The blue pigment will absorb the yellow light and the orange.

It now appears that all the colours have been absorbed by the object's surface, bar one – green – which is reflected and is seen by our eyes. By mixing blue and yellow, we arrive at green, see Fig 10.2(c). If this all seems a bit confusing, spend a little time working through and digesting its logic. By understanding the process, you can see the principles behind using some very strange colours to correct errors.

THE COLOUR TRIANGLE

Fig 10.3 shows the colour triangle. If all the primary colours are mixed together, we should end up with black, because all the light would be absorbed and none would be reflected. In practice because coloured pigments are imperfect, some light does become reflected, which leads to the familiar muddy brown we all ended up with at school. We can use the colour triangle to work out how to correct an unwanted colour cast.

The points of the triangle represent the primary colours (blue, red and yellow). The sides represent the colours produced when pigment of the primary colours adjacent to it are mixed. In the centre you can see an area of neutrality, where no particular colour seems to be present. This is the result of all three primary colours being mixed. A colour cast is corrected by applying the colour opposite to it in the triangle. For example, red is neutralized by green, yellow by purple.

FRENCH POLISHING

USING PIGMENTS

Figure 10.4 below is a before and after photograph that shows a piece of old oak furniture, the top of which was so damaged that it needed to be stripped. It was then stained with water-based stain using Vandyke crystals. The result is a brown-oak colour that is both more uniform and lighter than the rest of the piece. To both darken and create the variations in colour seen on the rest of the piece, pigments were used.

YOU WILL NEED:

- Artists' powder colour or oil paints.

- Raw linseed oil or gold size thinned 50/50 with white spirit or pure turpentine.

- Terebine (this is a paint drier and accelerates hardening of the oil or gold size).

You need to make a judgement about which colours to use, but for this task, raw umber, a little burnt umber and black were required. Black pigments are very powerful so you need to use them sparingly. The

Fig 10.4 Before (left) and after (right) view of the effect of pigments in oil on creating a matching distressed surface.

powder pigment or oil colour is liquefied with a small amount of white spirit before blending with the oil or gold size. It is difficult to give specific quantities of colour, because each case needs to be taken on its merits. Add a teaspoon or two of terebine per half pint (250ml) of pigmented oil.

Apply the colour to the surface with a soft rag and rub it into the wood. The colour remains fluid for quite a while so you can manipulate it over the surface to create areas that are darker or lighter than others. Pay particular attention to areas where you would expect an accumulation of dark grime over time, such as in the corners of mouldings, around handles and key escutcheons, and make sure there is some natural-looking colour build-up there. You also need to ensure that the colour is well rubbed into the work as you do not want heavy accumulations on the surface. Take your lead from the rest of the piece of furniture. You need to leave the work to dry for a day or so before polishing. If the surface is still tacky, wait longer.

You can create a similar effect by substituting oil stain for the pigments, especially if you are looking for an effect that is less 'cloudy'.

USING TINTED POLISH

Sometimes, it is after you start polishing that a colour imbalance becomes apparent. At this point you need to tint the French polish and effect colour correction after skinning-in and before bodying (see Chapter 7 on French polishing for the sequence of events). Spirit dyes or NGR stains can be mixed with transparent polish to produce the colour required. The problem is usually one where the colour cast is wrong. Mahogany and oak are often too red, or oak has a cold greenish cast. The colour triangle shows what colours should be used. Excessive redness can be toned down with a green tinted polish, while a cold green-brown can be warmed up with red.

YOU WILL NEED:

- Spirit dyes or NGR stains.

- Methylated spirits (meths).

- Pale transparent French polish, thinned in the ratio or two or three parts polish and one part meths.

If the spirit dye is in powder form, it needs to be dissolved in a little meths before mixing with polish. The powder may take some time to fully dissolve, so prepare this well in advance. Only mix it into the polish when it has fully dissolved. Use a freshly made rubber for this colour and apply the correcting polish using the 'bodying' method described in Chapter 7. You may need more than one coat to correct the colour cast.

It is tempting to make up a strong colour in the belief that it will work more quickly, but this can lead to problems. It is better to apply several pale-coloured coats where the corrective effect builds up slowly. If the colour in the polish is intense, you run the risk of creating the opposite effect – i.e. an unwanted colour cast of polish colour. The colour builds up very quickly because of the cumulative effect of adding layers. The first pale coat may not appear to make much difference, but the second coat will. There is a multiplying effect, so go easy and inspect the surface carefully in a good light.

GENERAL DARKENING POLISH

This creates a similar effect to that discussed under Using Pigments, on the facing page, except that the pigments are suspended in thinned French polish. Getting the colour of the surface right with stains and pigments is the preferred option, but if the result is still not satisfactory you can use this procedure to make a correction. It can only effectively be carried out on dark surfaces – e.g. mahogany, medium to dark oak, or darker shades of walnut.

YOU WILL NEED:

- Artists' powder pigments (not oil colour).

- Meths.

- Thinned garnet French polish (two parts polish: one part meths).

The aim of darkening polish is to give it a slight opacity and colour which effectively darkens the surface. Pigments are suspended in the polish, and so will have an obliterating effect.

Mix a little vegetable black pigment with meths to liquefy it and blend with the polish, ensuring that it is completely dispersed. Add a little reddish pigment (e.g. burnt sienna or burnt umber) to this mixture, after first dispersing it in meths, and completely disperse it. This should produce a slightly muddy brown.

Guidance on exact quantities of pigment cannot be given, as this depends upon individual circumstances. The colour balance of the darkening polish will be determined by the amount of darkening required. Sometimes the balance needs to be towards the red, and sometimes towards the black. This may not sound terribly helpful, but this is not an exact science. Experience very definitely improves your skill, and a highly developed colour sense will prove invaluable.

The darkening polish must not look like a paint, i.e. so heavily laden with pigment that it is a solid colour. It must still be fairly transparent because, again, you achieve the end result by applying it in thin coats. If there is too much pigment, the polish will dry as a solid obliterating coat, and will be quite rough.

Fig 10.5, overleaf, illustrates a before and after effect of darkening polish on a piece of medium oak veneer. The effect has been deliberately exaggerated for this photograph to show how dramatic it can be. The effect you are generally trying to achieve is a slight overall darkening.

VARNISHING

Varnishing presents a more difficult problem, as very few dyes will dissolve in the solvents unless water-based varnishes are used, in which case water-based aniline dyes are ideal. The very nature of varnishing also means that relatively thick coats are applied, so there is always the danger of over-colouring. In many cases the answer is to prepare some spirit aniline dye and mix it with a little transparent French polish, applying the resulting mixture with a rubber over the

Fig 10.5 The effect of a 'darkening' polish.

stained surface. When the colour is satisfactory you can varnish normally.

An alternative approach would be to mix a little oil stain into the varnish, or water-based stain if the varnish is water-based, so that you are effectively using a less intensely coloured version of a varnish stain, but you have more control over the colour and can build it up.

MODERN SPRAY LACQUERS

NGR stains can usually be mixed with the lacquer to colour it. As this is also thinning the lacquer, you need to ensure that the viscosity is not reduced to a level where the lacquer is too 'thin'. Include the stain when you are thinning to the correct viscosity. Base, or matching tints – i.e. pure colours such as red, blue, green and black – are available for use with spray lacquers and are matched to the type of lacquer. The same principle of not making the colour too intense applies as it is better to apply two thin coats rather than one thick.

CREATING A MODEL

There is a golden rule in woodwork which says: measure twice: cut once. The principle is clear – do not commit an irreversible action on your work without being sure that you are right. In woodfinishing, the principle is equally valid. Colour is an incredibly difficult area of work, so it is a good idea to create a 'model' of the colour you are trying to achieve, and then match your work to that.

To do this, you need a piece of the timber used in the work, or as close a match to it as possible, so you can build up the colour you want to achieve on that. This includes restoration work if a degree of trial and error will be needed. Once you have created this 'model', and recorded how you achieved it, you can commit yourself to colouring the work. Colour models are used a great deal in production work where new batches of colouring agents can be compared against the model to ensure consistency.

PAINTING OUT BLEMISHES

Fig 10.6 shows the sort of blemish that should be corrected using the painting-out technique. This ring in a French-polished surface was caused by a glass or cup with a wet base. In most cases, white ring-marks result from moisture entering the polish film and discolouring it, but here the object had been left on too long and the polish lifted off. It must be repaired with a colouring polish designed to paint it out, made up from dark polish, coloured with spirit dye, or NGR stain mixed with pigment for opacity. Figure 10.7 shows the paint being applied in short strokes along the grain on the affected area.

Fig 10.6 Polish and colour completely removed by a wet object on a French-polished surface. The light area is bare wood.

Fig 10.7 Rectifying the damage by painting it out with dyed polish and pigments.

Fig 10.8 Disfiguring damage caused by a cigarette burn on highly figured wood.

Fig 10.9 The repaired blemish. Artists' acrylic paint masks the worst of the damage, although damaged areas are often still visible to some degree, because of the change in the surface level which reflects light differently to the surrounding area.

A more difficult case of painting out is shown in Fig 10.8. Cigarette burns are a real challenge: it is difficult, maybe impossible, to mask the blemish in a way that will not be detected. The choice is very simple: you can leave the blemish – a very ugly scar – or you can reduce its visual impact by painting it out to blend more closely with the surrounding area. Even though it may still be noticeable because there is always a depression left after scraping away the badly scorched fibres, painting out may be the better alternative. Fig 10.9 shows the repaired blemish.

Artists' acrylic colours are ideal for this task as they are fast drying and you can get on with polishing quite quickly. You will need a good light for this work and view the results as you go along by looking across the surface rather than straight down at it.

- On figured wood (i.e. where there is a strong grain pattern) the blemish is masked by overlaying it with different colours to match the underlying surface. You need to begin by determining which colours to use. Look at the surface and you will see that there is a base colour that is usually the lightest of them. Thin a small amount of acrylic colour with water to a thin creamy consistency. Use a fine artists' brush to lay this colour down with short strokes along the grain. This will hide the blemish, but will leave a definite 'smudge'. Allow it to dry for a few minutes.

- Next, determine the next lightest colour and brush this on to the patch. You do need to be careful here as the aim is not to cover the whole patch, but to begin simulating the grain texture, or figure.

- There may be other colours that need to be overlaid, and these are done in ascending order of darkness.

In other words, you begin the process with the lightest colour and finish with the darkest. You will rarely need more than about three colours.

Allow plenty of time for previous coats to dry, and remember that the colours must be laid down with short strokes of the fine artists' brush, and should be in a similar pattern to the real pattern of the figuring. When the process is complete, allow a couple of hours to dry and seal in the colour with the appropriate polish.

DEALING WITH SCRATCHES

Deep scratches are easier to handle. Acrylic colours are good for this as well, but the paint must be thinned right down, to make it less opaque. Colour-out the scratch by painting along it (see Fig 10.10), then seal in with polish, applied carefully with a pencil brush. You may need to refinish the whole surface to blend it in.

Fig 10.10 Painting out a scratch.

Finishing Turned Work

Lathe-turned wood has its own special properties and finishing needs, and this chapter is dedicated to looking at these in detail.

HOLDING THE WORK

The main problem in finishing turned work is holding the item. Wherever possible, newly turned work should be kept on the lathe for finishing. By leaving the work on the lathe you can keep both hands free, so as not to ruin the finish by handling it. This is quite simple when dealing with between centres turning, but faceplate and chuck work can be a little more awkward. While between centres work can be placed on and off the lathe with relative ease to make way for other jobs, bowl and chuck work may tie up the equipment for a number of hours. It is a matter of planning ahead. Each case must be treated on an individual basis, but in many cases you should be able to delay the finishing process until all the turning has been completed.

STAINING

A great deal of turned work is left unstained, but there are occasions where you may need to colour the work, such as in restoration work where you have no choice but to match the colour.

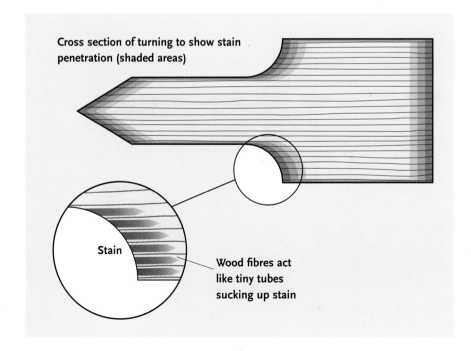

Cross section of turning to show stain penetration (shaded areas)

Stain

Wood fibres act like tiny tubes sucking up stain

Fig 11.1 Capillary action of short and end grain makes these areas of the work stain darker than the rest.

Water-based stains are not ideal for this type of work. The problem is that turnings have a very large proportion of short and end grain that absorbs far more water through capillary action than other areas, causing them to become much darker (see Fig 11.1, previous page). At the same time, the wood fibres will have been compressed by the machining and as soon as water comes into contact with them, they will have a natural tendency to swell and cause roughness. If water stains have to be used, carry out the grain-raising procedure first, smoothing the work while still on the lathe.

If at all possible, use oil or spirit-based stains, such as NGR wood dyes, but keep in mind potential problems of incompatibility with the final finish. (These problems are discussed in Chapter 5.) If you intend to use cellulose-based finishes, use NGR or non-strike dyes.

FINISHING MATERIALS

The finishes most commonly used by craft turners are: wax, oil, French polish, nitrocellulose and/or melamine, two-pack catalysed lacquers. Commercial work will be subjected to whatever the requirement of the job will be and is often sent to the client unfinished for fitting and finishing on site.

WAX

Waxing is a quick and attractive finish, producing a low lustre that allows the figure of the wood to speak for itself. However, it is not durable, and so will not stand up to a great deal of handling. The item will quickly become grubby and lose its initial attraction.

Carnauba is the traditional woodturners' wax, and it is bought in a stick or block form designed for woodturning. The block of wax is held against the work as it rotates at relatively low speed on the lathe (see Fig 11.2 a). Friction melts the wax, and by slowly moving the block from one end of the work to the other, it is distributed over the whole surface. The work is then burnished with a special polishing cloth held against the workpiece as it rotates at slow speed (see Fig 11.2 b). The polishing cloth is much safer than an ordinary cloth, which is likely to snag on the rotating item and to trap your hand in the rotating machinery, risking serious injury. A final buff with a polishing cloth, while the lathe is stationary, tidies it up and removes wood dust.

The problem with pure carnauba is that it is brittle and can chip off the work. Also, because the block of wax is hard (similar to a block of toffee), soft-textured woods can be damaged by the pressure needed to generate sufficient friction to melt it. A compromise is

WAX POLISHING

Fig 11.2 (a) Using friction against the wax block to apply the wax.

Fig 11.2 (b) Burnishing the waxed surface with a special polishing cloth, which cannot get caught in the machinery.

Fig 11.3 Melting and combining carnauba and beeswax in a double boiler.

to use a carnauba and beeswax (50/50 mix) block, which you can either buy ready-made or make yourself.

Use a double boiler to melt and blend the waxes (see Fig 11.3). Pour the molten wax into a suitable mould to cool and harden. Aluminium baking or take-away containers are ideal, as they can be peeled off easily when the wax has cooled and solidified.

The alternative is to use wax polish. Apply it with a cloth to the stationary workpiece (it is very easy to get a cloth trapped on a rotating item), then allow the polish to dry and harden for an hour before burnishing on low revolutions with wood shavings using the shavings technique described above. To finish, buff the stationary piece with a clean polishing doth. Some woods may need two or three more applications.

Some time and polish can be saved if you give the work a coat of sanding sealer first. Sealers are either shellac- or cellulose-based. Both contain a quantity of a chemically inert, fine white powder which allows abrasive paper to bite more effectively. Sanding sealer reduces the amount of wax that is needed, while at the same time sealing out dirt. The sealer is brushed onto the stationary item with a polisher's mop (see Chapter 7) or a similar soft-haired brush. Make sure there are no runs, which can be very difficult to remove once dry.

After allowing the work to dry, the surface is de-nibbed (i.e. the adhering dust particles are removed) using very fine abrasive (320 grit or finer) before waxing.

OIL

Richly figured woods look stunning when oiled, and apart from the fact that it is a durable finish, oil helps reduce drying out and cracking.

Any of the oils described in Chapter 6 can be used and applied in the normal way, but expect turned work to be thirstier because of the short and end grain. Tung oil is ideal because it is light and fast drying. Apply generously, perhaps with a soft-bristled brush, and allow a day to soak in. Burnish with a soft cloth (with the article stationary) or shavings (with the lathe rotating at low revolutions). There is a lot to be said for completely immersing the article in oil for a day or so before removing and wiping off the surplus and finishing off on the lathe. If you do this, put the piece to one side for a few days to allow the oil to harden.

The proprietary oils are probably better for gaining a good finish quickly but, if the object is to be used with food you must not use them, because they will taint the food; there are also substances in proprietary oils that will contaminate, such as terebene or similar drying agents. These articles must be left unfinished, or an edible vegetable oil can be employed. I always use one of the lighter oils, such as sunflower, safflower or rapeseed. They are so light they soak in rapidly and, being pale, they do not cause an appreciable colour change.

FRENCH POLISH

Use shellac-based sanding sealer to satisfy the initial suction of the wood. After an hour or so, it can be cut back and another coat applied. Two coats will normally be enough to produce a high, grain-filling build.

After cutting back the last coat, make a rubber of suitable size to fit the work and use this to build up the gloss with French polish, using the rubber (see Chapter 7) and rotating the work by hand (see Fig 11.4).

Once the polish has completely hardened for at least 24 hours, it can be burnished to a high gloss if necessary, provided there is no open grain that will end up trapping the cream and forming an unattractive white residue. Apply a proprietary burnishing cream on a small pad of cotton wool held against the workpiece

as it rotates at low speed (see Fig 11.5, on the facing page). Take care not to generate so much heat that the shellac melts and ruins all your hard work.

NITROCELLULOSE AND MELAMINE

Fast-drying lacquers based on nitrocellulose and/or melamine, with other synthetic polymers added, are ideal because the work can be completed quickly. A cellulose-based sanding sealer is brushed on, allowed to dry and then cut back with fine abrasive. A finishing coat (usually giving a gloss or satin finish) is applied and allowed to harden before burnishing with the lathe at its slowest speed.

If you want to cut back the sheen, you can burnish with wire wool (or nylon mesh abrasive) and wax polish (see Fig 11.6, on the facing page). The work is then hand-buffed with the lathe stationary.

These lacquers contain very powerful solvents and, if the piece has been spirit- or oil-stained, there is the risk of the colour bleeding out into the finish and ruining the look.

FRENCH POLISHING

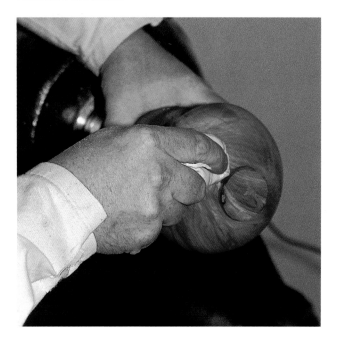

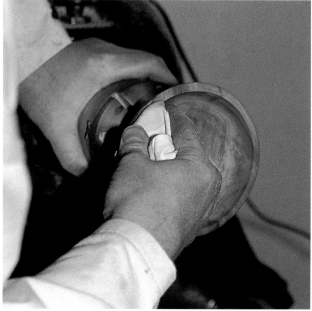

Fig 11.4 (a) Applying the polish with a rubber, rotating the lathe by hand.

Fig 11.4 (b) Polishing the inside of a bowl with the rubber.

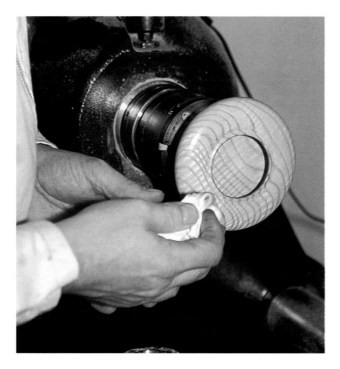

Fig 11.5 Use burnishing cream with the lathe set at lowest revs and use very light pressure.

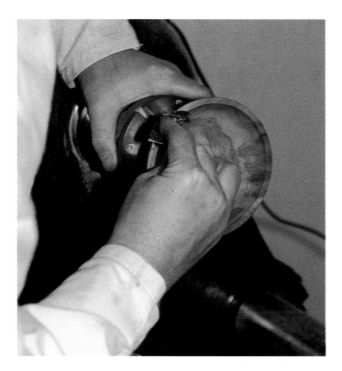

Fig 11.6 Dulling a high shine with abrasive and wax polish.

TWO-PACK CATALYSED LACQUERS

Sanding sealers are not necessary here, as the lacquer has a high build. Remember that once the catalyst has been added to the lacquer, the pot life is limited, and, above all, never put back unused lacquer into the original container. Follow the instructions for mixing lacquer and catalyst to the letter, as the proportions are quite critical. The first coat can be thinned with the special thinners provided in the lacquer kit to help satisfy the wood's suction.

Large items can be brush-coated. Follow the procedure described for nitrocellulose/melamine above, but allow more time for hardening, which is through chemical action rather than solvent loss. The product will give guidance here. Small items such as light pulls can be dipped, as shown in Fig 11.7, and hung up to dry; the lacquer should be thinned down a little more, as dipping leads to a heavier coating. Since the lacquer hardens by chemical action after the initial evaporation of solvent, the thicker coat should not lead to the problems of softness associated with finishes that rely entirely on solvent evaporation for hardening.

Catalysed lacquers can be burnished on the lathe at slow speed, but allow a couple of days for the catalytic action to completely harden the finish.

Fig 11.7 Dipping small items in catalysed lacquer.

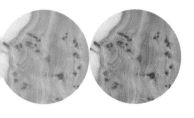

Protecting and Preserving Timber

Timber is a remarkably durable material when environmental conditions are right but, if the conditions are not right, wooden structures can be destroyed in a frighteningly short time. This chapter is concerned with those factors which lead to its destruction, and with how timber can be protected.

It is an unpleasant fact of life that any naturally occurring organic material will have at least one living organism capable of using it as a food supply. Wood is no exception to this rule. The main agents in this process are insects, usually the larval stage, and fungi. The two are frequently linked, in that the tunnels created by the burrowing larvae allow the entry of fungal spores, often carried into the wood on the insect's body.

A less obvious risk to wood is strong sunlight. Long-term exposure to ultraviolet radiation results in a degrading change in the structure of wood.

INSECT ATTACK

Fungal attack causes the moisture level of wood to increase, and in these conditions the wood can undergo secondary infestation by insects and other invertebrates, such as weevils or woodlice. This wildlife is unwelcome, but in these circumstances they must be considered a clear indication of the irretrievable state of the wood. These animals can only handle wood as a source of nutrients when it has reached a well-rotted state resulting from the fungal

Fig 12.1 Wet rot will reduce timber to a soggy, fibrous mass.

attack. Under this onslaught the wood can be reduced to a pile of black moist powder, with only strands of the harder areas remaining intact (see Fig 12.1, on the previous page).

The most obvious signs of insect infestation are the exit holes, the points where the adult insects have chewed their way to the surface of the timber before flying off. The adult stage is normally short-lived and, after mating, the female lays her eggs on the surface of the timber. After the eggs hatch, the young larvae burrow their way into the wood to begin their destructive life cycle.

This part of the life cycle can last for several years, depending upon the species, during which time they tunnel their way through the structure. 'Worm holes' are in fact the exit holes caused by the mature insect escaping, but they are not a true indication of the extent to which the wood has been excavated and its structure weakened.

Nevertheless, a large area covered with exit holes should be taken as an indication of very serious damage to the timber's structure. Fig 12.2 illustrates in general terms the life cycle of wood-boring insects.

Different species tend to differ only in the length of time each stage takes.

COMMON FURNITURE BEETLE

This is one of the commonest of timber pests and is, or has been, present in most old houses and a great deal of old furniture. The adult beetle emerges during the summer months, an event often marked by the appearance of fine wood dust (frass). The beetles only live for a couple of weeks, and mate very soon after emerging.

The female lays her eggs in crevices, on end grain, or on rough timber, never on smooth surfaces.

When buying or inspecting old furniture, it pays to concentrate on inspecting the backs, the inside of frames and other hidden areas, as these will be favoured by the beetle. The larval stage lasts for at least two years, depending on the temperature, humidity and type of timber. They love oak and walnut, in particular. The ideal conditions for furniture beetles are a temperature of around 22°C (70°F) and air humidity of around 50%. Older houses without central heating present favourable conditions for infestation.

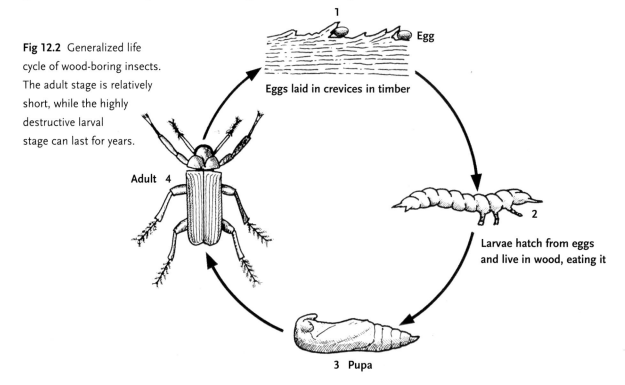

Fig 12.2 Generalized life cycle of wood-boring insects. The adult stage is relatively short, while the highly destructive larval stage can last for years.

1

Egg

Eggs laid in crevices in timber

2

Larvae hatch from eggs and live in wood, eating it

3 Pupa

Adult 4

The exit holes of the furniture beetle are about 1.5–2mm ($^1/_{16}$in) in diameter. Recent holes are light in colour on the inside, while older ones tend to darken with age and accumulated dirt. Frass will be evident nearby, as well. You may also see a number of very small holes (less than 1mm) situated nearby; these are caused by a group of small insects called chalcids, that prey on the furniture beetle larvae. Their larvae have the charming habit of living as parasites on the beetle larvae. The adult chalcid either emerges through an old beetle exit hole or creates very small ones of its own. Fig 12.3 shows the typical exit holes of the furniture beetle and the adult insect.

COMMON FURNITURE BEETLE

Fig 12.3 (a) An adult common furniture beetle

Fig 12.3 (b) Exit holes and honeycomb effect caused by the burrowing larvae. While the surface of the wood may look intact, the internal structure is weakened by the labyrinth of tunnels.

DEATHWATCH BEETLE

A related species to the common furniture beetle, this is one of the larger wood-boring beetles. The eggs are laid in April or May, and the larvae may take five to ten years to complete this stage of the life cycle before the adult beetles emerge. As you might expect, the exit holes are large, at 3–5mm ($^1/_8$in to almost $^1/_4$in) 0diameter (see Fig 12.4).

LONG-HORN BEETLES

This is a group of related species (70 species in Britain) that attacks structural timbers (see Fig 12.5, on facing page), their generic name coming from their long antennae. The 'house long-horn' beetle feeds on dead timber, and this is how it can find its way into house structural timbers. However, it is not very common, fortunately. Easy control is achieved by not introducing bark-covered timber into the house.

DEATHWATCH BEETLE

Fig 12.4 (a) The adult deathwatch beetle.

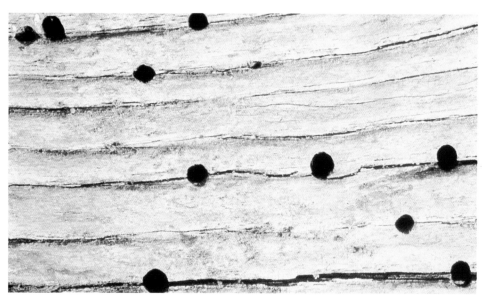

Fig 12.4 (b) The large flight holes caused as the new adult makes its escape from the wood.

LONG-HORN BEETLE

Fig 12.5 (a) The characteristic long antennae of the adult long-horn beetle.

Fig 12.5 (b) Exit holes made by long-horn beetles are large.

PREVENTIVE MEASURES

Any felled timber that has spent a good deal of time lying around, especially if it has seen a spring and summer in that state, should always be treated with suspicion and never brought into the house if you can avoid doing so. It is relatively easy to import pests into the house in the form of firewood, but removing the bark and sapwood first helps, as these are the parts vulnerable to attack.

Other preventive measures include the maintenance of a dry environment. Centrally heated houses are, somewhat paradoxically, a fairly hostile sort of environment. While the temperature may be ideal, central heating usually brings a reduction in the air-humidity levels, and reduced wood-moisture levels with it. Regular inspections of structural timbers and furniture may help you spot an attack at a relatively early stage.

TREATMENT

While prevention is always better than cure, it is not always successful, and so we need to rely on eradication. The brief descriptions of life cycles given above would seem to indicate that the spring and summer months are quite crucial to the insects, as during this time the adults mate and the females lay their eggs. These are the months when you should be vigilant in looking out for the tell-tale signs. Examine all surfaces of the wood, especially the hidden areas, such as the backs of cabinets, for new holes. If you find an area where the holes look particularly light in colour or there is fresh frass around, assume an attack.

Large-scale attacks to structural timbers by furniture beetles or attacks by deathwatch or house long-horn beetles should be dealt with by one of the pest control organizations. The chemicals required to eradicate pests are highly toxic, and a large-scale operation needs very close supervision of the way in which they are used. Small-scale attacks, such as those associated with furniture, are quite easy to deal with.

The aim of pest control is to prevent re-infestation and to destroy any larvae that are still in the wood. The holes appear because an insect has burrowed its way out, not the other way around, so it may appear that we are bolting the stable door after the event, but there are other considerations. For example, there may be larvae present in the wood at a different stage of their life cycle, and treatment will, we hope, kill them. Treatment of nearby furniture is a good idea, because of the obvious danger of cross-infestation.

TREATING FURNITURE

There are a number of proprietary woodworm treatment products, and there is not much to choose between them in terms of efficiency, as they are all strong insecticides.

The vulnerable areas to be treated are those that are not normally visible such as the backs, the inside of the tops of legs, and tops and bottoms of carcasses. Show wood is rarely the source of the problem, but may exhibit the effects with unsightly exit holes. Unpolished wood should be treated by brushing the fluid on to it and letting it soak into the surface.

The best way to treat woodworm is to inject the fluid into the flight holes: this achieves greater penetration, and also makes it more difficult for any remaining larvae to spread, or for new larvae to enter via the old exit holes. On a relatively small item of furniture where the area affected is fairly small, this presents no problem. Woodworm-killer containers come with a spout that acts as an injector, and this can be pushed into the holes and the can squeezed to force the fluid in (see Fig 12.6). It is not necessary to inject every hole, as the tunnels frequently interconnect. Inject one hole for every square inch (2.5cm) or so, but be careful as, while you inject one hole, the fluid squirts out of another – possibly directly into your face.

Any other furniture in the room should be given some protection by painting the solution on to the backs and unpolished internal surfaces. This will help to reduce the risk, or scale, of cross-infestation.

Because these substances are toxic, it is necessary to observe the simple rules of hygiene. Wash your hands after use, and try to limit contact with the skin. Do not attempt to spray the liquid because the overspray will release the toxic chemicals into the atmosphere that you and others are breathing.

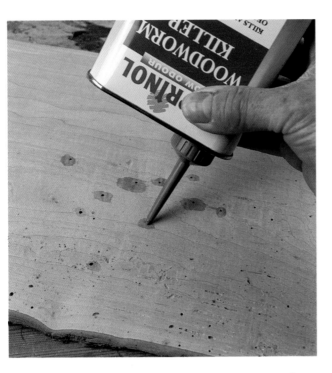

Fig 12.6 Inject flight holes with woodworm fluid. You need only inject one hole per square inch (2.5cm, or so), as the tunnels are interconnected and the fluid will travel along them.

In addition to the woodworm fluids, there are special anti-woodworm wax polishes containing insecticide, and it is worthwhile dressing all show wood with this, especially where they show flight holes. Finally, because of the extended life cycle of the larvae, it will be necessary to keep an eye on furniture for a couple of years, to ensure you have eradicated the problem. It is worth repeating the process of painting woodworm fluid onto unseen timbers during the spring following the initial treatment.

FUNGAL ATTACK

Fungi are responsible for decomposing organic matter and releasing materials for recycling in nature. They are not welcome when their action causes timber to disintegrate before our eyes. The problem may be compounded by the softening effect on the wood fibres that encourages animal pests, such as weevils and woodlice, to invade and cause further destruction.

PROPAGATION

Fungi propagate by spores which are dispersed in the air from sometimes spectacular outgrowths, or 'fruiting bodies' (see Fig 12.7, overleaf). These spores can lie dormant for very long periods before springing to life again when conditions for growth are right. The most important condition is that of timber moisture. Most fungi that attack timber prefer a moisture level of around 30% to 50%. The most vulnerable timbers are those that are in permanently damp or wet conditions. Exterior constructions such as garden building, decking, fencing timbers in contact with the soil are obvious targets. Dry timber is naturally durable and can last for between 20 and 30 years in good condition, with a little help. Providing recently soaked wood is dried out fairly quickly, there is little danger of serious fungal damage as a result of a single event, but repeated or extended periods of high moisture levels will eventually lead to wood rot, unless adequate protection has been afforded.

There are two generic types of 'rot' that we refer to when describing and dealing with fungal attacks – wet and dry rot. Dry rot is particularly feared because of its rampant nature and they way it can quickly destroy 'dry' structural timbers.

'WET' ROT

The first sign of fungal attack often takes the form of patches of blue-black discolouration caused by mildew-type fungi. The spectacular discolorations in so-called 'spalted' timber (and also 'brown oak') are caused by the chemical staining of the wood by the fungus as it feeds on it.

The damage is caused by the way fungi feed. The fungus literally digests the wood fibres by releasing enzymes into the body of the wood which break down the cellulose and other complex compounds before absorbing the nutrients back into itself. The wood becomes soft and spongy and its moisture level rises, making the conditions for further deterioration ideal, so the process is almost self-perpetuating. Finally, the structure of the timber is destroyed and it crumbles away as a soggy, fibrous mass.

DAMAGE CAUSED BY WET ROT

Fig 12.7 (a) Dramatic example of a fungal fruiting body called a 'bracket'. This will produce millions of spores, each one capable of causing a new fungal infection somewhere else.

Fig 12.7 (b) The small orange 'blobs' are the fruiting bodies of a slime mould that has taken hold of a cross-member on a poorly maintained wooden gate.

Fig 12.1, on page 111, shows a typical example of the damage caused by wet rot, as this process is known. The so-called 'slime moulds' are able to permeate right through the internal structure of the timber with no external signs of their presence until they produce bright yellow, orange or red pin-head spores carrying growths on the surface. These release spores into the air, which carries them off to new sources of food.

In extreme cases it will be necessary to cut away the affected timber and replace it with new, sound wood. That said, the progress of wet rot is relatively slow when compared with the rampant spread of dry rot, which is normally associated with timbers that appear to be completely dry, or very nearly so.

'DRY' ROT

The fungus that causes dry rot, *Merulius lacrymans*, will thrive in timber with a moisture level as low as 20%. The problem is that once the fungus has established itself it can spread to dry timbers (hence the name), because it can survive on the moisture gained from the original damp timber. The fungus can spread very rapidly in two ways: first, it will generate millions of spores that are dispersed through the air; second, it can spread by sending out tiny fibres, called hyphae from its main body, to seek out new sources of nourishment – i.e. timber. The hyphae are capable of growing over several metres of masonry and cement in its search, even though these provide no nourishment whatsoever. The main body of the fungus will supply the hyphae with the nourishment they need until new timber has been located. Once new timber is located, it will establish itself there and start the process of propagation all over again. The consequence of this is that while wet rot is relatively slow to spread, dry rot can be rampant and spread with frightening speed (see Figs 12.8 a and b overleaf).

TREATMENT

Dry rot infection is best dealt with by a professional builder or a company that specializes in pest eradication. The treatment usually involves a radical removal of timber adjacent to the attack, because you can never be too sure of how far the hyphae or spores have reached and this means large-scale repair work. The liberal application of fungicides, both on the remaining timber and the new replacement timber, ensures that eradication has been completed.

Small-scale wet rot attacks can be dealt with on a DIY basis. The affected areas need to be cut away and replaced with new, sound timber. It is important that all affected wood is removed, as any fungus left behind will become the source of further destruction. This means that you will need to cut back well beyond the obvious area of infection and will need to remove some good, sound timber as well to make sure. Finally, the timber will need a coat of preservative, to provide protection against future attack. Preservative should be applied to the exposed surfaces after cutting away the damaged area; next, cut patching timber to size and apply preservative before fitting.

PREVENTIVE MEASURES

As always, prevention is better than cure. Bearing in mind that fungi generally attack damp timber, it is obvious that the best preventive measure is to ensure that timbers remain dry, either by eliminating sources of moisture or by ensuring that vulnerable timbers are given adequate ventilation. Timber treated in this way will rarely be attacked by fungi associated with wet rot, but regular inspection is advisable. Furniture is rarely attacked by fungi, as the moisture level in the timber, even in the worst domestic environments, is unlikely to reach a critical level.

Timbers that are likely to be constantly wet and exposed to moisture will need preventive treatment. These are essentially structural and external timbers, and the section overleaf on Preservatives provides more information. But, in the first instance, when undertaking external construction projects, including fencing, factory pre-treated timber should be used because the level of protection is enhanced through the use of preservatives applied under pressure to improve penetration. Ongoing maintenance usually takes the form of an annual ritual (chore?) of preservative application.

Fig 12.8 (a) The characteristic appearance of dry rot. Notice the fibrous hyphae on the surface which are designed to spread the fungus into new areas of 'fresh' food – i.e. neighbouring timber. The hyphae can bridge significant barriers in search of 'food'.

PRESERVATIVES

The choice of preservative depends on a number of factors, and some questions need to be addressed before making a choice, as a 'horses for courses' rule applies here. Manufacturers tend to formulate their products for specific purposes, so you need to ask yourself:

- Is it for internal or external use?

- Will I be painting the wood or finishing it in some other way after the preservative has been applied?

- What decorative properties do I require? In other words, am I applying this to a garden fence which is made of rough timber, or to a new front door to my house, which must have a high-quality and resilient finish?

There is a confusing array of products. A trip to the local DIY superstore will confirm the problem, with shelves filled with preservatives specially designed for one purpose or another. By answering the three questions set out above, you can narrow down

12.8 (b) The extensive damage shown here can occur within a frighteningly short period.

the choice to a few products appropriate to the circumstances. You also need to check what the product is actually designed to do.

STRUCTURAL TIMBERS

The oldest and cheapest preservative is creosote, which is based on coal tar. While it is effective, it is also toxic to plants, wildlife and pets. Modern formulations have to be manufactured to adhere to environmental and health and safety standards and are designed to be used as 'maintenance' products on timbers that were originally pre-treated prior to sale. These timbers were treated with preservative in a pressurized environment to improve penetration and on their own will afford protection for up to 20 years or more, provided they are not subject to permanent or long-term saturation with water, or cut into during construction projects (which will expose unprotected surfaces).

You cannot automatically assume that all products designed for exterior timbers are going to protect the timber against fungal or insect attack. A number of products are designed to be decorative and have few preserving qualities other than providing some waterproofing through oil and wax ingredients. These products are designed to be used over timbers that have been factory treated with preservative (Fig 12.9).

Almost all of these products are strongly pigmented, to provide additional protection from the sun's ultraviolet radiation, which is damaging both to the wood and the preservative itself. UV is an effective decomposer of organic material and the high-energy rays break down organic chemical bonds, leading to the eventual destruction of the timber. Special UV-absorbing pigments are present in the product to reduce this effect. Some will also provide additional protection from fungal attack.

If you are using timber that has not been pre-treated, that will be subject to the extra demands of constant water saturation, is buried in the ground, or has been cut during structural work, additional protection is needed. A dedicated preservative product should be used. These may be colourless or be lightly

Fig 12.9 The decorative finishes for external timbers may have a limited preservative effect, relying very much on UV-absorbing filters and water-resisting oils and waxes.

Fig 12.10 A demonstration of the capillary action of end grain. Use this feature when applying preservative to vulnerable timbers, allowing time for it to soak in.

coloured as much to help you identify where you have applied the preservative as to provide a decorative effect. If you can soak cut ends or end grain for a few hours, all the better, as capillary action will carry preservative deeper into the wood with time (see Fig 12.10).

SHOW WOOD

A preservative is of little value if it does not penetrate the surface of the wood, and the deeper the penetration, the greater the protection. If the surface also resists water penetration, then all the better. Many of the preservatives described above do offer some protection from this, thanks to the waxes and oils used in their formulation, but they may not provide the decorative properties of varnishes.

So-called 'wood-stain' products are designed to provide a hard decorative finish to smooth wood such as doors and windows. They provide the properties of a physical barrier, protection from UV and some limited protection from fungal attack. They are pigmented moisture-permeable varnishes (see Chapter 8), and the latest generation of these varnishes is water-based, which makes them fast drying (which allows two to three coats to be applied in a single day), and safer to use (i.e. less volatile vapour to breathe in).

Since protection can only be provided to that portion of the wood containing the preservative, these materials are probably not as effective as preservatives (except against surface mildew and algae), especially if the varnish coat becomes damaged, allowing both moisture and fungal spores to penetrate. The best protection is provided by treating the wood with a colourless preservative prior to using the wood-stain varnish, if it has not already been factory treated.

Fig 12.11 shows a door treated with a modern 'wood-stain' product. No more than two or three coats should usually be applied, or they will become less permeable to internal moisture. Properly applied, such varnishes will last for up to six years with conscientious maintenance (see Chapter 8). There is one negative feature of these products, in that the pigments used frequently lead to a slight opacity, especially as far as the darker tones are concerned. The result of this can be that the natural figuring of the timber is sometimes partially obliterated.

Fig 12.11 An external door case treated with an exterior 'wood-stain' product that provides UV and water-penetration protection.

A Guide to Refinishing

If woodfinishing is considered by many to be fraught with difficult decisions about what product or procedure to use in which circumstances, maintaining or repairing an existing finish raises even more potential difficulties. This chapter looks at some of the common areas of difficulty and describes solutions to the problems they give rise to. Some of the problems have been covered elsewhere in the book (for example Chapter 10 on colouring), so general principles and specific decision-making and processes in two distinct areas – furniture and general joinery – are discussed in this chapter. The pros and cons of stripping are also described, as well as the general principles.

The repair of finishes on furniture is generally more problematic than that of general joinery, because the decisions are tied up with notions of what constitutes an approach that maintains the integrity of a piece.

FURNITURE

Knowing when and how to refinish furniture is often regarded as a problem area. It is not simply a question of knowing the techniques, it is a matter also of knowing how far to go. Common sense and care will go a long way to solving the problems, but there are several key questions to ask before attempting to repair furniture, and this includes colour and polish:

- Is this a valuable antique or 'collectable'? Yes to this question demands that you step back and consider the impact of any repair you undertake on the integrity and monetary value of the piece. A bad or misjudged repair can reduce the value of an antique.

- How serious is the damage? This is a difficult question to answer, because the response is entirely subjective, but it must be asked because the underlying judgement concerns the degree to which the damage is disfiguring and/or difficult to live with. Furniture is used, not hung on a wall or hidden away, so some wear and tear is to be expected, but is this normal wear and tear on a well-cared-for piece, or is it trauma damage?

- Do I have the skills and know-how to undertake a repair that retains the integrity of the piece? The crucial judgement is about the extent to which you can restore the piece to a condition consistent with its age and general condition. The section on Patina below explores this in more detail.

PATINA

The questions in the last section are mostly concerned with the quality of the surface on furniture, commonly referred to as patina. This concept is not an easy one to define with any precision, but a general description of patina will make an adequate definition, as much is in the eye of the beholder. After years of exposure to light, the atmosphere, and hand polishing by successive 'caretakers', the surface appearance and texture changes. Dark woods fade and light woods darken as a result of exposure to light, and there may be variations in the colour across the surface. The texture of the surface changes to a mellow gloss rather than the bright gloss of the original state. There may be undulations in the surface due to the natural movement in wood over decades (or centuries).

Figure 13.1, below, shows part of the top of a mahogany chest of drawers. Examples of patination include the variation in colour across the surface and the relationship between colour variation and the figure of the mahogany veneer. There is a very clear colour difference here, but the original repair was skilfully executed, with well-matched figure. The colour difference is the result of the differential fading. Is this patina? The answer is 'yes' because it is the natural result of age rather than trauma – even if the original repair was used to correct trauma damage to the service. The repair itself is old and provides further evidence of age. The veneer repair is an example of a 'wear and tear' repair.

If you look more closely at Fig 13.1, though, you will see real damage to the surface – scratches, water spots and a narrow crack that runs the length of the top. What is less clear is that the surface is generally dull as well. If the overall appearance of the surface can be enhanced without resorting to stripping and changing its underlying optical qualities, then this is a legitimate refinishing activity.

Fig 13.1 Patina: mellow sheen to the surface and variation in colour testify to the age and authenticity of a piece.

The importance of patination cannot be ignored in restoration work, as it is an indicator of age and, by implication, of authenticity. Absence of patina makes collectors suspicious and reduces the value of the item in the saleroom. However, a line must be drawn between genuine patina – the mellowing of a surface through use, generations of hand polishing and exposure to light – and grime or real damage. Patina is a property of the polish film and wood surface, a part of the furniture, not something on the surface that can be removed by cleaning. For example, it is generally accepted that minor dents and scratches are legitimate forms of patination, since they are not really disfiguring, but a cigarette burn is damage, which it is permissible to repair.

Stripping old polished surfaces and refinishing them, even using traditional methods and materials, will destroy valuable patina and should only be carried out under extreme circumstances by someone with the skills to recreate or preserve as much of the original patina as possible.

The bottom line is, wherever possible, avoid stripping an old surface; there are usually better alternatives, especially if the old surface is basically sound. Decisions about the level of imperfection that can be tolerated need to be balanced against the damage to the integrity of an antique or collectable that may result from enthusiastic over-restoration. The rule of thumb in restoration work is, therefore, to apply the least drastic remedy first, then progress to increasingly more drastic measures as necessary. Above all, do nothing, if you can – and do nothing that will destroy the integrity of the piece.

CRITERIA FOR STRIPPING

Start from the premise that stripping is unnecessary and undesirable unless:

- The old finish is badly damaged, i.e. flaking off or very badly worn, and so is highly disfiguring. The item is much reduced in terms of value and utility.

- The old finish is known to be a modern lacquer;

i.e. it cannot be repaired because a good bond between old and new finishes will not be obtained.

- The colour of the wood has been bleached by strong sunlight, producing a dirty grey hue that is often restricted to one area of the piece which contrasts sharply with it, and needs to be restored by recolouring the badly bleached areas with the rest.

Valuable pieces should be stripped and refinished by a professional restorer. Other items can be refinished by the amateur without losing intrinsic value, but even here it is not always necessary to strip. If the old finish is basically sound, just as it is in Fig 13.1, opposite, it can be improved. Some guidelines on stripping furniture are described later in the chapter (see page 132).

IDENTIFYING AN EXISTING FINISH

A prerequisite for the decision-making process in refinishing is to know the identity of the existing finish. It is unwise to make assumptions about a finish on the basis of the age of the piece alone, as someone in the past may have replaced the original finish with something else – polyurethane varnish, for example.

Modern finishes are difficult to identify positively, as they will not soften if subjected to rubbing with a cloth moistened with solvents. They are non-reversible, and this fact alone can be used as a means of positive identification.

If you do not know what finish has been applied, Table 4, below, explains how to test with solvents and scrapings to arrive at an answer.

The table works by a process of elimination, asking questions and guiding you to others. Start at 1, and if the answer is that the finish will not soften with methylated spirits (meths), you are told to move to 2, and so on, until you arrive at a final answer. When testing a surface with solvents or by scraping, choose a small and inconspicuous area. The solvent should be applied with a soft clean cloth, but begin by cleaning it with soap and water, to remove grime that could confuse the result of the test.

TABLE 4: FINISH IDENTIFICATION KEY

Step	
1	Finish softened with meths FRENCH POLISH OR SPIRIT VARNISH Not softened with meths GO TO 2
2	Finish softened with white spirit GO TO 3 Finish not softened with white spirit GO TO 4
3	Finish feels waxy and smears when rubbed with a finger; will scrape off when scratched with fingernail WAX Surface feels oily smooth, but will not smear or scrape off with fingernail OIL
4	If scraped with blade of sharp knife, finish will produce tiny flakes with some dust POLYURETHANE VARNISH If scraped with blade of sharp knife, forms a white dust GO TO 5
5	Will soften with cellulose thinners NITROCELLULOSE LACQUER Will not soften with cellulose thinners CATALYSED LACQUER

WAX AND OIL FINISHES

These are easily 'repaired'. Marks caused by heat, moisture and handling are removed by wiping over the surface with white spirit or pure turpentine, allowing it to dry again and then re-coating it with wax polish or furniture oil.

FRENCH POLISH

CLEANING AND REVIVING

A neglected polished surface will be dull with accumulated dirt and old wax. If it has been regularly polished with an aerosol polish or with wax pastes over a long period of time, the surface can become very greasy and dull, with grime trapped between successive layers of wax polish. These surfaces will benefit from the use of a reviver after a good clean.

Clean the surface with a solution of one teaspoon of washing soda in a pint (500ml) of warm water, using a well-wrung-out chamois leather. The solution must not be much stronger than this as the soda may act as a stripping agent. Allow to dry, and then test for any remaining deposits of wax by rubbing the surface with a fingernail. Wash the surface again, if necessary, until all dirt has been removed. After drying there will still be a dullness, and possibly some whitish streaks, which is emulsified residue. A reviver will remove these and brighten up the surface. Recipes can be found in Chapter 16.

Apply the reviver sparingly with a pad of stockinette, working a small area at a time with circular movements. As the area brightens, change to straight strokes and finish off by buffing with a clean piece of stockinette. Revive the whole surface in this way before finally buffing it all with a clean pad.

REPOLISHING

If, after all this, the French polish is still dull, or even shows signs of wear, it will need to be repolished to bring back the shine. It should not be necessary to strip, unless cleaning and reviving has shown the surface to be badly damaged. An old trick is to use shoe polish on furniture to mask the fact that the original polish has been damaged. Cleaning and reviving will reveal that deception. If the original polish is intact, the following steps will bring it back to good condition:

- It should be prepared first by cutting back with 600 grit wet-or-dry paper, used wet. A little detergent in the water acts as a wetting agent and makes the task easier. The aim is to key the surface in preparation for rebodying.

- Once the surface has been cut back in this way, rebody with French polish thinned a little (one part of meths to three of polish), and finish by stiffing (see Chapter 7).

- The surface will be very bright and glossy, like new. To recreate the effect of years of hand polishing, leave the polish to harden and settle for a day or two before dulling a little with fine nylon mesh abrasive and wax polish (see Chapter 7 for details of this method).

Of course, all this assumes that the French polish is without serious blemishes. There may be marks and other defects that require special treatment.

RING MARKS OR CLOUDY AREAS

White marks are caused by water or heat, and can be easily removed or, at least, reduced:

- Mix some cigarette ash to a paste with raw linseed oil, and apply the paste with a finger wrapped in a cloth. Apply a fair amount of pressure, and rub along the grain over the ring (see Fig 13.2, on the facing page). Faint blemishes will begin to respond quite quickly, while heavily marked areas may need two or more applications over a period of a few days.

- Wipe off any surplus oil afterwards, and clean the whole surface with a reviver. The marks may not disappear altogether, but they will look much less obvious.

DEALING WITH WHITE RING MARKS

Fig 13.2 (a) Before – these marks are disfiguring but if the general condition of the finish is good, attempt to reduce it without stripping the surface.

Fig 13.2 (b) Linseed oil and cigarette ash treatment. Apply a fair amount of pressure with your finger along the grain.

Fig 13.2 (c) After: the ring mark is considerably reduced, and in many cases will disappear altogether.

Some dark rings are caused by very hot dishes which have been allowed to rest on the surface and the heat has discoloured the wood. Scorch marks can only be treated in the same way as cigarette burns, i.e. by stripping off the polish, scraping the scorched fibres, and painting out the blemish (see Chapter 10).

Dark marks may also result when water penetrates the polish and stains the wood. A frequent cause of this is over-watered plant pots, the over-spill going unnoticed until it is too late. The only cure is to:

- Strip the old polish and bleach out the stain with oxalic acid or 20 vol. hydrogen peroxide (see Chapter 5, Staining and Bleaching).

- Restain, if necessary, and polish as required. This action is drastic, however, and careful consideration should be given to it: if you can live with the marks, do so rather than risking ruining a good piece of furniture.

Desks and bureaux are often found with small black (or red or blue) rings caused by ink (see Fig 13.3):

- A little weak oxalic acid can be applied to the ring after stripping off the old finish (see Chapter 5), to bleach out the ink marks.

- Clean off the acid afterwards with a weak solution of bicarbonate of soda, and buff dry.

Other ring marks show up as areas of polish that have been removed completely. This blemish is often caused by alcohol on the bottoms of glasses that dissolves the polish. These areas will need to be recoloured and polished (see Chapter 10).

SCRATCHES

Very minor scratches can be darkened by rubbing over with a little raw linseed oil and wiping off the surplus, or by rubbing the exposed face of a broken brazil nut over it. The natural nut oil will penetrate the scratch

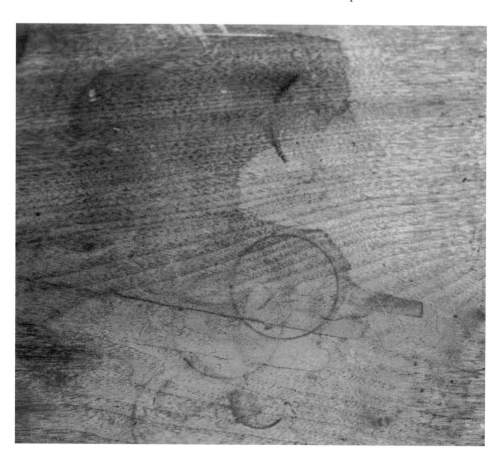

Fig 13.3 Ink stains are typical of writing desks and bureaux.

and darken with exposure to the air. If the scratch is very white:

- Mix a little powder pigment of an appropriate colour with French polish.

- With a steady hand paint out the scratch.

- Once the pigmented polish has dried, repolish the surface to disguise the blemish.

You must take care in touching up, or it will show up as an obvious ridge or smudge. (Chapter 10 gives more information on colouring.) Major scratches may necessitate stripping and repolishing.

FLAKING OR CRAZED POLISH

There is not a lot you can do here, other than strip and repolish, as the old finish is disintegrating and will not successfully accept new polish. An alternative to using proprietary strippers is the process called reconstitution. This method is a more controlled way of removing damaged French polish and is described below.

RECONSTITUTING A FRENCH-POLISHED SURFACE

This process works by gently dissolving French polish and redistributing it over the surface. It has a number of advantages over the total stripping approach of proprietary strippers in that it is more controlled, does not necessarily result in the total removal of polish, and helps retain much of the original colour of the surface.

You will need fine nylon mesh abrasive pads and meths. French polish has alcohol as its solvent so the approach is to gently dissolve the polish film and redistribute it. It is particularly effective in dealing with crazed, badly scratched or discoloured polish.

- Pour meths into a container and dip the face of the nylon mesh abrasive into it. Squeeze out surplus meths so that the mesh is damp.

- Gently rub the surface of the work with the dampened abrasive, working along the grain. The polish will gradually dissolve. You will find it necessary to recharge the mesh with meths as it dries out.

- Continue working over the surface until the blemishes disappear. Allow the surface to dry and harden again for a few hours.

- Once the surface has dried and hardened, it will have a white residue and will feel slightly rough. Quickly wipe over the surface with a cloth moistened in meths to clear the white away so you can see the surface and check for missed blemishes.

- Finally, after a few hours have elapsed to let the residual polish harden again, gently rub along the grain with fine nylon mesh abrasive to remove any roughness.

- Rebody the work with French polish.

The beauty of this method is that it dissolves and redistributes polish rather than stripping the surface completely. This means that much of the original colour and underlying patina remains. It is a little messy because the abrasive mesh becomes sticky with dissolved polish, but it does mean that you need only work the surface sufficient to ensure that the blemish is removed, but that the bulk of the original polish remains on the work. In short, it spreads the polish around. However, if you continued to work the surface, the method will also strip it of polish, but not as cleanly, perhaps, as a proprietary stripper, so you may have difficulty getting stain to take on the resulting surface.

SYNTHETIC LACQUERS

A synthetic lacquered surface is not so easy to repair, and you may well find that the only action to take will be to strip it down and repolish. However, there can be a serious drawback to stripping catalyzed lacquers: they do not react well, if at all, with proprietary strippers. You may find it necessary to hand this work over to a commercial stripping company that is equipped with the facilities to deal with the rather dangerous chemicals needed to strip this kind of lacquer.

JOINERY

Many of the ethical issues associated with furniture are not a problem here, as a general rule, unless you are dealing with architectural restoration, of course.

VARNISHES

If the varnish film is mostly sound, with perhaps a little flaking and some bare patches here and there, the surface should be washed down, avoiding bare areas, allowed to dry, rubbed down with 240 grit abrasive and re-coated with one or two coats of varnish (follow the procedure for smoothing down between coats as outlined in Chapter 8).

Where varnish stains are being used and the surface has bare areas, even small ones, you may need to strip the surface completely and treat it as a new surface for refinishing. If you do not do this, an uneven colour may result.

Peeling varnish is an indication of progressive loss of adhesion, and it is wise to strip the old finish before varnishing again.

MICROPOROUS VARNISHES

The important thing to remember is that a microporous (MVP) varnish should not be used over a non-MVP, such as polyurethane or yacht varnish, because its permeability will be lost. It is essential to strip off these other varnishes first.

If you are refinishing a surface with MVP varnish, then use one coat over the existing MVP varnish. Alternatively, strip off the old and apply no more than two coats. The reason for this is that the thicker the coating of varnish, the less effective it is at allowing water vapour to pass through.

PRESERVATIVES

These tend to weather and fade naturally (if coloured), and, provided they are not a varnish-based compound, can simply be re-coated. If you want to use one of the new generation of water-based compounds on wood that was originally coated with solvent-based material, such as creosote, you must make sure that the old material is well weathered. Depending on the conditions, re-coating should take place every couple of years to ensure maximum protection.

STRIPPING

TYPES OF STRIPPING COMPOUNDS

The wide range of products on the market make it difficult to be precise about the exact use of each, but there are general principles which are covered in this section of the chapter. They all work by softening the finish to a state that enables the worker to scrape it away.

Varnish and paint strippers can be placed in one of three broad categories:

NON-CAUSTIC, SOLVENT-BASED

The active ingredient is usually methylene chloride with alcohol as the carrier. There is often a thickening agent to help the stripper adhere to vertical and shaped surfaces. Fumes can be dangerous in confined spaces so very good ventilation is essential, and if you have chronic respiratory problems, or are sensitive to fumes, use a respirator. The term non-caustic refers to the absence of caustic soda, which is a traditional stripping agent.

NON-CAUSTIC, WATER-BASED

This is similar to the solvent-based product, except that the carrier is water rather than alcohol. It also has a thickening agent to improve adhesion to the surface being stripped.

CAUSTIC, WATER-BASED

These products are less common these days because of their chemical nature and the discoloration they often cause on oak and mahogany, in particular. Caustic soda is the active ingredient and the product is sold in powder form to be mixed to a paste with water. Caustic soda is highly soluble in water, but generates a large amount of heat. The powder is mostly made up of a chalky material that creates the paste. The paste is spread quite thickly over the item to be stripped. After stripping, the residue of caustic soda must be neutralized with white vinegar.

COMMERCIAL STRIPPING

Stripping your own furniture is a messy business, so sending the work out to a commercial stripping company is a realistic option. There is a balance of cost and risk to be weighed up, though. The time saved by you can be employed doing something else more constructive or creative, and this may be worth the money paid to the stripping company.

On the other hand, horror stories abound about the problems of 'dipping' furniture. In the past, there was less professionalism about in this arm of the industry, but improvements in the technology and professional standards of operators make this less of an issue. Things to consider before choosing a company are:

- Do you know anyone who has used them and can recommend their services?

- How good is their customer service when you contact them? For example, do they provide you with adequate answers to general questions about the process, and do they give adequate specific advice about the furniture you want to send them? This includes advice about after-care.

- Do they belong to a reputable trade association to whom you may take any complaints if the company fails to provide satisfactory service or to address your complaint?

- What technology are they using?

These questions are, of course, common sense ones that you ought to ask of any company you want to engage for any work on your property, but the last question is a crucial one because there is a 'horses for courses' element to this. There are two principal 'technologies' in use by commercial companies: solvent-based processes, and caustic processes. These reflect the description explained in the last section.

SOLVENT-BASED DIPPING PROCESSES

The company will be using solvents rather than water-based chemicals (e.g. methylene chloride). Since water is not used, except to rinse off the work to neutralize and remove residue, the furniture is left to soak in solvents that do not attack or dissolve traditional animal glues. There is less risk associated with sending veneered work, although some caution is needed because of the rinsing-off stage. The chemicals should not discolour hardwoods, either.

Because the overheads associated with the technology and materials is more expensive, this will be reflected in the price of the job.

CAUSTIC DIPPING PROCESSES

This is the traditional process of dipping the work into vats of caustic soda, sometimes heated to speed-up the process. In the hands of skilled and professional operators this should not be a problem, but there are things for you to consider. The process means that the item will be in prolonged contact with water, which is bad for veneered work in particular and antiques in general. Operators working to high professional standards will tell you this and may refuse to take your work. In any event, you should ask about the process they use and what after-care will be needed.

The point of after-care is important because, when the item is returned to you, it will still be damp. Following the dipping process, the work will be washed down with water to remove residue and wash away the caustic solution. You must let the work dry out slowly before attempting any refinishing. This may take a week or more. You run the risk of excessive and rapid shrinkage if you try to speed this up, with the usual result that cracks or disfiguring splits can appear.

As the work dries out, you may notice a whitish residue appear, which is caustic soda residue. Wiping over the area with white vinegar in water should deal with this, but you may have to repeat the application.

Fig 13.4 Preparations for stripping furniture. Remove doors and drawers, and remove handles. Dismantling the work makes it easier to manage the job in sections and get to awkward areas. Put down plenty of newspaper to catch the drips.

PREPARATION FOR STRIPPING

Put down lots of newspaper on the floor beneath the work, adding enough for an area for splashes. Have an old bucket filled with cold water to hand so that, as the softened varnish is lifted off the wood, it is dropped into the bucket, out of harm's way.

- Protective clothing should include heavy-duty rubber gloves of industrial quality (as household gloves would dissolve), eye-protectors, and a respirator with a gas cartridge, if you are working in an enclosed area without adequate ventilation, or the work period will be quite long. Plenty of ventilation is needed because of the volatile nature of solvent-based strippers. Of course, precautions also need to be taken to reduce the possibility of fire.

- Fig 13.4 shows an item of furniture being prepared for stripping. The door has been taken off and the drawer pulled out. Door and drawer furniture, including hinges, must be removed to reduce obstructions. Each dismantled 'bit' effectively becomes another separate item to strip, so the whole work can be sectioned into manageable areas.

- Do not use shavehook scrapers when removing the softened polish, as they have a tendency to dig into the wood; instead, modify an old cabinet scraper or wallpaper scraper, as shown in Fig 13.5. 00 grade wire wool, or coarse nylon mesh abrasive, can be used to remove material from awkward places such as carvings and mouldings, because a scraper will simply dig in and damage the wood.

GENERAL PROCEDURE WITH SOLVENT-BASED STRIPPERS

On large work, tackle each section of the work separately. If you attempt to apply stripper and work the entire piece in one operation you run the risk of letting stripper dry onto the surface before you get a chance to scrape it away. You will only have to do the work all over again, which is an obvious waste of time and materials.

- Brush the first coat of stripper on like paint. This will provide a key, by roughening the surface.

- After a couple of minutes, apply a very generous second coat. Don't be mean with it, either: it is

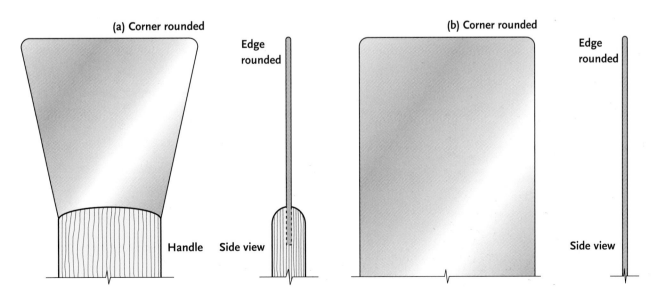

Fig 13.5 Modified wallpaper knife **(a)** and cabinet scraper **(b)** for use in furniture stripping. Rounding over the edges reduces the risk of the tool digging into the surface.

expensive stuff, but skimping will mean that you you having to spend more time and use more stripper. There should be a very substantial layer of stripper on the surface, but not so much that it runs all over the place. Work the stuff well into crevices and corners with a stabbing action of the brush.

- Leave for at least 15 minutes on French-polished or varnished surfaces. Test by scraping a small area with the scraper, to see if it has softened sufficiently to be peeled off. If not, leave for another five to ten minutes before testing again. For thick layers of paint and cellulose lacquers, you may need to leave it for up to an hour.

- The stripper may begin to dry out partly through evaporation and partly through thickening with the softened finish. If this happens, gently dab on another generous layer of stripper.

- When the finish has been softened, use the scraper to 'peel' it off flat surfaces, along the grain, and drop the gooey mess into the bucket of cold water. Use the wire wool or nylon mesh abrasive on carvings and mouldings and, as it becomes clogged, drop it into the water to neutralize and make it safe.

- If there are many layers of paint, thick varnish or some cellulose lacquers, you may need to repeat the process as the stripper can only work on the surface and may not penetrate very deeply.

- When stripping is complete, the residue must be neutralized. Each product will recommend what to use, but these tend to be water, white spirit or meths. If possible, avoid using water on veneered work as this risks excessive shrinkage and splitting of the veneer. Apply the neutralizer generously with nylon mesh abrasive and scrub the surface to remove residue.

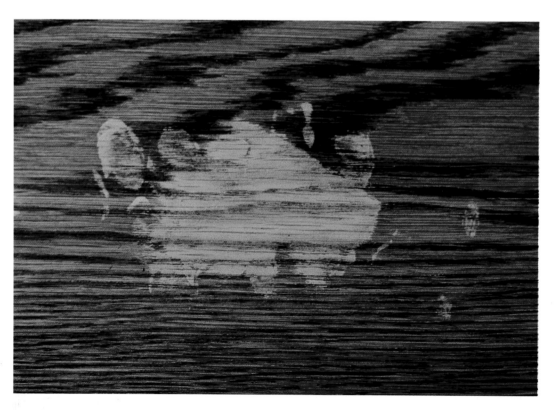

Fig 13.6 The light area shows where the stain has not taken because of incomplete stripping of the surface.

- Finally, wipe over the work with clean rags to remove the residue and allow the work to dry overnight.

Sometimes a finish will resist the action of strippers, even to the point where they have no effect whatsoever. This occurs with some of the catalysed lacquers, and there is little you can do about it; stripping with abrasives is one possibility, but this is laborious and is only feasible on flat surfaces. You may have to resort to commercial stripping companies.

TREATMENT AFTER STRIPPING

After stripping, the wood is treated as if it is a new surface, and can be smoothed with abrasives, stained and repolished. If water has been used to neutralize the stripper the surface may be a little fuzzy due to raised grain, but usually very little preparation is needed. Use only a fine abrasive (240 or 320 grit).

Veneers present a tricky problem in that they are very thin, and extra care needs to be exercised: use a 320 grit abrasive, and work cautiously to remove only raised fibres, not the veneer itself.

If you find that a stain will not take properly, this is probably due to incomplete stripping. The stain simply refuses to become absorbed by the surface, or there is patchiness where it is absorbed in some areas but not in others (see Fig 13.6, on the facing page). The only solution to this problem is to use the stripper again, and to rub over the work with 000 steel wool or nylon mesh abrasive after about 15 minutes. The stripper must be neutralized as described above. A rough and ready test to see if stripping is complete is to lightly sponge the surface with water before staining. If the water beads, then there is still some finish on the surface. The water should soak into the surface. Use water sparingly on veneers.

Fig 13.7 Flaking or cracked finishes cannot be retrieved. Stripping and refinishing is the only reliable option.

14 Special Paint Effects

Walk through the paint section of any major DIY store and you will see a bewildering array of products for special paint effects. This simply reflects the burgeoning interest in the more exciting decorative effects that were once the sole territory of the professional decorative artist. Now we all have access to the materials and techniques that were once so jealously guarded and, in keeping with the philosophy of the book, this chapter aims to demystify further this area of woodfinishing.

Of course, the effects described have many other applications, and do not have to be restricted to working with wood. An important point to consider and remember, though, is the notion of appropriateness. While a large, flat area of wall may benefit from some bold and exciting effects, furniture is of a much smaller scale and may demand more restraint and subtlety. In truth, there are no set rules that cannot be broken so, if it works, do it.

More than any other finishing technique described so far, paint gives you an outstanding opportunity to experiment, safe in the knowledge that disasters can be painted over. This does present a problem to writers, because the possibilities, while not infinite, are too numerous to cover in a single work. This chapter makes no attempt to approach the impossible by being a comprehensive discussion of all the possible techniques, but the main tools, materials and techniques are described in a way that will equip the reader with the knowledge and confidence to develop skills and to experiment.

Most specialist paint effects rely on building up layers of colour over a base coat, and considerable time and effort goes into completing a project. You will want the finished product to be durable. This is particularly true of furniture where regular and hard use may be made of it. Always finish with two coats of varnish, except for floors where the paint should be protected with up to five coats of varnish.

TOOLS

PAINT AND VARNISH BRUSHES

Often regarded as a basic tool, the temptation is to skimp on the quality of paint and varnish brushes. This is a mistake for two reasons:

- A good finish is partly determined by the quality of tools you use. Cheap brushes shed bristles that become lodged in the coating and spoil it. Cheap brushes also slow you down because they do not hold as much paint or varnish and it is more difficult to 'lay off'.

- How much value do you put on the quality of what you do? You owe it to yourself to use the best tools and materials you can afford, as they will help you develop your skills more effectively, and give you satisfaction in your work. This 'feel good' factor is important in any craft work.

ANATOMY OF PAINT AND VARNISH BRUSHES

You will need to keep two separate sets of brushes: one for applying paint or coloured glazes and washes (see Glazes and Washes, page 142), and another for applying the protective, clear varnish coats. Once a brush has been used to apply colour, it is useless for clear varnish because residual colour or paint particles in the brush can find its way into a varnish coat. If you can run to it, invest in a third set of brushes for applying coloured glazes only.

Figs 14.1(a) and (b) illustrate the key factors that distinguish a good brush from a bad one:

- Long, fairly soft and flexible bristles.

- The bristles should be set into the stock in three rows to give a high bristle density.

- The bristle tips should be split and feathered at the ends and tapered to give a slight dome across the brush width.

- The bristles should be secured into the stock with a strong gauge steel or copper ferrule.

This quality of brush will hold more paint, varnish, or glaze and ensure that it will be 'laid' onto the surface smoothly and evenly, without brush marks (which might become obvious later, when a coloured glaze is laid over it).

THE ANATOMY OF A PAINTBRUSH

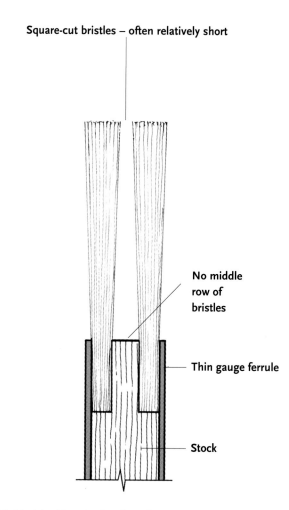

Three rows of good quality bristles split and feathered at their tips

Square-cut bristles – often relatively short

No middle row of bristles

Steel ferrule of strong gauge

Thin gauge ferrule

Stock

Stock

Fig 14.1 (a) A good brush has a generous crop of high-quality tapered bristles, set in three rows in the stock.

Fig 14.1 (b) A bad brush often has short, square-cut bristles. The stock is usually narrow to cater for the smaller amount of poorer-quality bristles.

Fig 14.2 A range of artists' brushes will be needed in your toolkit.

SYNTHETIC BRISTLE BRUSHES

There are some very good-quality synthetic bristled brushes on the market that seem to meet the requirements listed above. However, while they do perform very well for general-purpose painting, they are not suitable for specialized work that will be subject to close scrutiny.

ARTISTS' BRUSHES

Artists' brushes are used to manipulate small areas of coloured glazes and washes. Again, you should buy the best quality you can afford, made of sable (or high-quality synthetic bristles, as these will behave in a similar way to sable). You will need a variety of brush sizes and bristle lengths for different purposes. Figure 14.2 shows a small collection of suitable brushes. Sign-writers' pencil brushes, also come in very useful, as they have significantly longer bristles than others and have the wonderful property of being both flexible and easy to control for precision work.

SPECIALIST TOOLS

You will need other tools to manipulate colour over a dry or wet base colour and you can acquire them when you need them. The tools listed below form a core kit that will allow you to undertake a wide range of effects. They are easy to find in the major DIY warehouse stores or specialist paint shops, although they can be expensive items in some cases:

- Natural sponges

- Stipple brush

- Dragging brush

- Softener – for blending coloured glazes and softening outlines

- Feathers – for putting in the fine veins in marbling.

- Home-made combs – for creating a coarse-combed, or grained effect.

MATERIALS

BASE COLOURS AND FINISHING VARNISH

Painted finishes require appropriate and meticulous preparation of the surface as do any of the other finishes described in this book, including creating a base colour over which other decorative effects will be created. This will normally be a single colour using a standard paint. Some of the effects described here will require either an oil-based or a water-based paint, depending on how colour will be manipulated.

WATER-BASED EMULSION PAINT

For some work, emulsion paint is used, as its absorbency can be used to 'grab' subsequent layers. Emulsion paint tends to be good for producing very brushy effects, such as colour washing.

EGGSHELL PAINT

Where a colour has to be manipulated and blended over another, such as in marbling, the base colour needs to have an eggshell finish.

PROPERTIES

Eggshell has a low lustre, but has a smooth surface over which glazes and washes can be floated and manipulated with ease. You could use either oil- or water-based paint, but with a caveat. Oil-based paints have better flow characteristics and so it is easier to create a smooth surface with few, or no brush marks. Water-based paints are generally not quite so accommodating, and you need to pay particular attention to this. The advantage with water-based paints is, of course, their speed of drying. While oil paint will need overnight drying, water-based paints will be ready after a few hours in a warm environment.

Matt paint, including undercoat, is not suitable for this type of work because the surface is slightly rough (difficult to see, but it is this property that makes it matt) and so glazes do not float over the surface quite so easily. Gloss paint has too high a sheen, and glazes may puddle and break up rather than flow as an unbroken film.

BS4800

There is a group of standard colours that are based on strictly controlled combinations of defined pigment colours. The purpose of this British Standard was to create a range of colours that are identical, irrespective of manufacture or medium. The value to designers is obvious. A designer can specify a single colour for paints and fabrics using the BS4800 code and know that the products supplied will be consistent. In DIY terms, this is not important, but BS4800 colours are frequently specified in contract work.

VARNISHES

Many painted effects, and any that will take some handling and wear, must be protected by varnish. Where varnishing is specified, oil- or water-based products can generally be used irrespective of the finish, provided you have left enough time for the painted effect to dry completely. As at least two coats should be used, and as many as five for floors, water-based varnishes have the edge for speed of drying.

GLAZES AND WASHES

GLAZES

A glaze is any transparent colour with a drying time sufficiently slow to allow the colour to be manipulated over the ground. A good glaze can be manipulated for around 20 minutes, far longer than standard paint. Traditional glazes (called scumble glazes) were oil-based, as only this medium could remain 'open' for the time required. Technology has moved on, and there are now water-based scumble glazes.

Glazes can be bought ready-coloured or colourless. The latter is obviously more useful for making up your own colours, but pre-coloured glazes do have the advantage of consistency. If you run out, then another container of the same colour is going to be so similar, even from different batches, that any slight difference will be unnoticeable. If you make up your own colour, prepare more than you will need because you cannot afford the risk of running out. This is clearly wasteful. However, making up your own colour does give you many more creative possibilities.

You can make your own glazes – oil- or water-based, and recipes are given in Chapter 16. Oil glaze is based on linseed oil thinned with turpentine or white spirit and with a little terebene (paint drier) to help the oil dry hard. It can be coloured with artists' oil colours or paint tints that can be bought at any DIY store. Home-made water glaze is simply wallpaper paste made up to the consistency needed for lightweight wallpaper, and then coloured with artists' water-based paints or paint tints.

WASHES

A wash is thinned water-based paint. Thinning emulsion or artists' watercolour paint with water has two effects. The obvious effect is that it becomes very fluid and so has to be applied thinly to prevent runs. The second effect is that the colour is transparent or translucent, depending on the degree of thinning. As a wash has to be applied thinly, there is a third consequential effect – it dries quite quickly. This last effect makes it different from a glaze in terms of how it is used. It is difficult to manipulate a wash in the same way as a glaze.

PIGMENTS AND ARTISTS' COLOURS

ARTISTS' PIGMENTS

There can be some confusion over the difference between pigments and paints. Pigments are the basic colouring materials in powder form. Traditionally, they are finely ground coloured minerals that need to be mixed with a binding agent, such as linseed oil or gum arabic, which dries to hold the pigment in place on the work. Pigments should not be confused with artists' powdered watercolours, such as poster paints. In this case, the pigments have been blended with the water-soluble binding agent, dried, and then ground. If you mix these with water and allow them to dry, they will form a solid colour. Pigments, on the other hand, may appear to form a 'paint' when mixed with water but, once dry, they revert to being a powder again and can be swept away. Pure pigments are useful colouring agents because they can be mixed with any binding agent to form a paint.

OIL COLOURS

Artists' oil colours are composed of pure pigment ground into linseed oil to form a soft colour paste. This is now a paint because, when brushed onto a surface, the oil will react with the air and harden over time, binding the pigment together and bonding it to the surface. Oil colour can be thinned with white spirit or pure turpentine to create a liquid – in effect a simple glaze. Obviously they cannot be mixed with water, nor can they normally be mixed with any water-based product. Oil colours can be used to tint oil glaze (known as scumble glaze). The more you thin oil colour, the more transparent and pale it becomes (see Fig 14.3).

WATER-BASED COLOURS

While oil colours are relatively simple products, artists' watercolours are less so. For a start, there are several types of watercolour in common use: watercolour, gouache, and acrylics. Acrylics are the most useful product for the methods described in this chapter, because they provide strong colour and are the water-based equivalent of oil colour – with a distinct advantage. Acrylics are fast drying. While oil colour will be used to tint oil glaze, you can use acrylics to tint water-based glaze.

Fig 14.3 Thinning artists' colour progressively increases transparency and paleness.

PREPARING COLOURS FOR USE IN GLAZES

Oil and acrylic colours have the consistency of soft butter and will not easily mix with the glaze medium straight from the tube. You need to mix acrylic with a little water, or oil colour with white spirit or turpentine, so that it is fairly fluid. Only then can it be successfully mixed with the clear glaze (see Fig 14.4).

SURFACE PREPARATION

NATURE OF THE GROUND

It is a mistake to assume that paint will mask surface blemishes. Careful surface preparation is as important to paint as French polish. This is especially so when glazes or washes will be used, as these tend to pool in uneven areas, and even in brush marks left in the base colour. The effect of this pooling, slight though it may be, is that the blemishes are made obvious to the viewer.

NEW, UNFINISHED SURFACES

The standard preparation processes described in Chapter 4 apply here. It is not usually necessary to go for the mirror-smoothness required of fine French-polished work, but all blemishes must be removed as described in Chapter 4. This includes filling cracks and chips. Finally, apply a coat of wood primer, which seals the surface and eliminates excessive absorption of the main colour coats. Allow the primer to dry thoroughly. The process can be speeded up by using one of the water-based primers which dry quickly and, in a warm environment, will allow you to continue painting within a few hours. You can use oil-based paint over them.

OLD, COATED SURFACES

PAINT

Old, painted surfaces can present you with a bit of a dilemma. If the surface is painted already, and it is sound, a simple wash-down and rub-over with fine abrasive paper to provide a key will be enough to ensure a good bond with your new paint. Gloss paint needs a heavy rub-down with abrasives to dull and key it.

There is a problem, though: you must ask yourself whether the quality of the old surface is sufficient to ensure a perfectly smooth coating with new paint and glaze? More often than not, the answer is no. The old paint is frequently chipped and may be brushy or thickly applied in patches, giving a very treacly

PREPARING COLOURS FOR USE IN GLAZE

Fig 14.4 (a) Thinning artists' colour to liquefy it.

Fig 14.4 (b) Mixing colour into the glaze.

appearance. This is often made worse by the fact that there are many layers of paint that have been applied at intervals over the years.

You have to make a decision: strip the surface or not? In a book of this nature, the advice will be to strip off the old finish to ensure a good flat surface to work on. Once stripped, and sanded to make it smooth again, prime the surface after repairing blemishes.

VARNISH AND LACQUER

These are also best stripped off. You might get away with giving the work a good wash-down and a key, but you run the risk of not getting a good bond, in which case the paint will chip easily. You could use 'liquid sandpaper', which creates a key on the surface by roughening it. This product is very effective in producing a good bond with the surface and, when it has dried and hardened, you can paint over it.

GESSO

Gesso has a very long pedigree. It was originally made of fine chalk (whiting) and glue size (usually rabbit-skin glue) and applied to the surface hot. As it cools, the gesso gels and finally hardens. Its purpose is to act as a primer, and because it is heavy-bodied, it forms a thickish layer. Layers can be built up to fill the grain (especially in coarse-grained wood). Finally, when fully hardened, it can be sanded smooth with fine abrasive paper (e.g. 240 or 320 grit). It is at this point that something miraculous occurs. The matt and somewhat granular surface takes on a mirror-smoothness, like polished marble, to create a flawless surface to paint on (see Fig 14.5).

This is the purpose of gesso. It is used as a base for painted effects where a very fine finish is required. Paint can be applied directly to wood (assuming it has had a coat of primer first), but the surface texture of the wood will often show through, particularly where there is a strong figure or open-grained texture.

Traditional gesso is interesting to make, but it is time-consuming and messy, so modern materials have been harnessed to create a synthetic gesso based on the same fine chalk (whiting), but with acrylic medium as

Fig 14.5 Applying gesso.

the binder. It dries quickly to a very hard finish and is very easy to use. Simply brush it on and allow it to dry. Apply several coats to build up the surface before sanding smooth.

PRINCIPLES OF COLOUR MANIPULATION

APPLYING YOUR BASE COLOUR

The base colour forms the background, but its final appearance will be affected by colours painted over it, and by the way those colours are manipulated over the surface. This is the important property of the base colour. It needs to be selected so that the overlaid colouring materials can either be 'glided' over it to blend them (i.e. eggshell paint, which is not absorbent) or so that it will grab subsequent layers to create a brushy effect (i.e. water-based emulsion paint).

COLOUR OVER COLOUR

Glazes and washes are used over the base colour to create a variety of effects. The principle is the same whichever is used and whatever effect you are trying to achieve. While the base colour is invariably opaque, glazes and washes are meant to be transparent, or at least translucent, depending on the effect. This results in the base colour showing through, albeit modified by the overlying colour. The level of transparency is an important part of how to achieve the final effect.

COLOUR BLENDING

Other effects described in this chapter rely on blending different-coloured glazes on the surface. Effective cloudy effects are created this way, and if the glazes have a high level of transparency, very sophisticated effects are created by building up layers of blended colour. Figure 14.6 shows an example of colour blending, where one colour graduates into another. This form of graduation is brought about using softeners – very soft-bristled brushes, the tips of which are gently stroked over the wet glazes to blur the edges.

Fig 14.6 Different-coloured glazes blended over a solid, opaque base colour, is typical of marbling.

TECHNIQUES

COLOUR WASHING

MATERIALS

The base colour is water-based matt emulsion paint. A thin wash of colour is brushed over the base to create a brushy texture, similar to the effect used on the walls in the picture on page 138. The wash is made by thinning matt emulsion with three to four parts water (by volume). The colour wash may be a strongly contrasting colour, in which case the effect is very dramatic, or it may be a slightly different shade of the base colour, which creates a more subtle shaded effect.

METHOD

1. Paint on the base colour taking care to ensure a good surface finish. Allow the paint to dry completely.

2. Charge a clean brush with the colour wash and squeeze the surplus off the bristles against the side of the container. Brush the wash all over the surface, using long strokes in random directions. Figure 14.7 (a) shows the effect which is quite startling if the colours are very different. Allow to dry.

3. If a more subtle effect is required, one or more further coats will lead to a mottled effect (see Fig 14.7 b).

4. The work can be protected with a couple of coats of clear matt varnish if required.

STIPPLING

MATERIALS AND TOOLS

Stippling is more effective if a glaze is used over an eggshell base colour. Oil- or water-based eggshell and glaze are fine for this. However, if you are quick, you might experiment with emulsion paint. The only difficulty is that it is not easy to manipulate emulsion paint over an emulsion base.

COLOUR WASHING

Fig 14.7 (a) The first coat of colour wash produces a very startling, brushy effect.

Fig 14.7 (b) Subsequent coats of colour wash result in a more subtle, mottled effect.

The tips of a stipple brush are gently pressed into the wet glaze to provide a texture. Figure 14.8 shows a stipple brush.

METHOD

1. Apply the base colour, but be sure that there is a fine finish, as brush marks tend to show through a glaze. Allow to dry thoroughly.

2. Quickly apply a thin coat of glaze over the base colour. On large surfaces you may have to do this in sections that you can complete within the short time it takes for the glaze to start to go off.

3. Take the stipple brush and lightly dab the bristle tips in the wet glaze using a stabbing action. Cover the entire surface of wet glaze to create the effect (see Fig 14.9).

4. Allow to dry and protect with varnish.

Fig 14.8 A stipple brush.

Fig 14.9 The stippled effect.

SPONGING

MATERIALS AND TOOLS

There are two basic methods of sponging: 'sponging on' and 'sponging off'. 'Sponging on' uses a natural sponge dipped in paint and lightly pressed onto the base colour, leaving behind an impression of the sponge's texture. This technique is commonly used to sponge water-based emulsion paint onto an emulsion base colour, although a more transparent effect is gained by using glaze over eggshell, which results in a strongly textured pattern (see Fig 14.10 a).

'Sponging off' creates a more subtle effect where an eggshell base colour is coated with glaze and a sponge is then pressed into the wet glaze, lifting off some of it (see Fig 14.10b).

THE SPONGE

Natural sponge is traditionally used because of its texture and durability. Synthetic sponges are not as responsive or springy and tend to leave a distinct outline of their shape. The texture of synthetic sponges is also very uniform, which is reflected in the pattern generated.

Natural sponges are hard and brittle when dry so need to be soaked in water first. The sponge swells, softens and becomes springy. After squeezing out as much water as you can, use the sponge damp – even with oil-based glazes.

SPONGING

Fig 14.10 (a) Sponging on creates a strong texture.

Fig 14.10 (b) Sponging off creates a more subtle effect.

METHOD

SPONGING ON

1. Apply the emulsion base colour and allow it to dry.

2. Hold the sponge in the palm of your hand and dip the face into the second colour. Carefully remove heavy deposits of paint by wiping the face gently on the edge of the container.

3. With a light 'pecking' action, dab the sponge over the surface. The best effect is created by overlapping the dabs slightly, to prevent obvious edges. Recharge the sponge as the paint becomes exhausted.

4. If the sponge becomes sodden with paint, wash it out and squeeze out the surplus rinsing water before continuing.

5. For an even more dramatic effect, you could intersperse sponged areas of one colour with a second or even third colour – just experiment.

SPONGING OFF

1. Paint the surface with an eggshell base colour, which should be as flat and even as possible.

2. Dab the clean sponge firmly into the wet glaze. This will remove some of the glaze and leave behind a mottled effect. Work the sponge over the surface quickly, before the glaze begins to go off.

RAG-ROLLING

MATERIALS AND TOOLS

This is another very simple, but highly effective technique. Like sponging, there are two approaches: ragging on and ragging off. In ragging on, colour is put onto the base colour by rolling a crumpled rag over the surface. In ragging off, the rag is rolled over wet glaze, which removes some of it to create a more subtle effect. See Figs 14.11 (a) and (b).

RAG-ROLLING

Fig 14.11 (a) Ragging on creates a wildly random pattern of colour.

Fig 14.11 (b) Ragging off creates a surface reminiscent of mottled leather.

The rag used can be any textile that can be crumpled up into the palm of the hand, leaving a creased and folded face. Experiment with different textiles to see the effects they create. The larger the pad of fabric, the quicker it will be to cover the surface, and it will probably result in a much bolder pattern than that gained with a smaller pad held tightly in the palm.

The technique is also messy, and you will need plenty of fabric so that you can replace pads as they become soaked with paint. Remember, that it must be an emulsion base with any water-based ragged colour, or an eggshell base with glaze.

METHOD

RAGGING

1. Paint on the base colour and allow it to dry.

2. Crumple the rag in your hand and dip the face into the second colour. Remove any drips and heavy deposits on the side of the container.

3. Dab and roll the rag on the surface to create the pattern. Recharge the rag as it dries out.

RAGGING OFF

1. Paint the surface with an eggshell base colour.

2. Make up a crumpled rag prior to applying the coloured glaze, and roll the rag over the glaze so that you create a pattern by removing and displacing glaze.

DRAGGING

MATERIALS AND TOOLS

Eggshell base colour and glaze are used for this technique, which involves dragging the bristles of a paintbrush (or better still a special dragging brush – see Fig 14.12) through wet glaze to create a striated effect similar to wood grain.

METHOD

1. Paint a thin coat of glaze over the eggshell base colour.

2. Take the paint or dragging brush and drag the bristle tips through the glaze in a straight line.

3. When one line is completed, create another stroke adjacent to the first, with a very slight overlap so as not to miss any areas, as these will be obvious.

MARBLING

The techniques described so far are examples of producing layers of colour one over another. The next two, marbling and tortoiseshelling, are examples of the effects achieved when different coloured glazes are manipulated and blended on the surface.

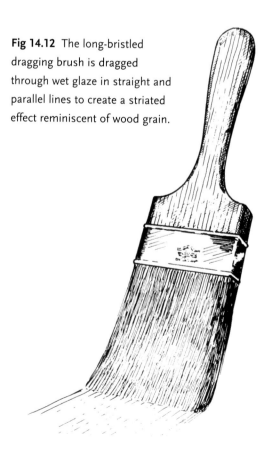

Fig 14.12 The long-bristled dragging brush is dragged through wet glaze in straight and parallel lines to create a striated effect reminiscent of wood grain.

STAGES IN BUILDING UP A MARBLED EFFECT

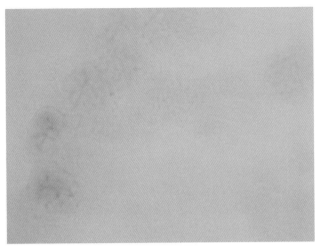

Fig 14.13 (a) Grey glaze sponged onto wet clear glaze.

Fig 14.13 (b) Grey glaze is softened to create a clouded effect.

Fig 14.13 (c) White veins created with an artists' brush, or with a feather moistened with white spirit.

Fig 14.13 (d) Grey veins painted in and softened to create the classic marble look.

MATERIALS AND TOOLS

Marbling is characterized by softly mottled colours with strong veins of colour running through, just like the real thing. Exponents of the craft can recreate any type of marble, but there is insufficient space here to describe all of them. Instead, the focus is on the general principles of marbling, which will allow you to experiment. I describe the method of creating the ubiquitous grey/white marble with dark veins, as this explores the use of all the generic techniques.

The base colour will always be eggshell and the marbled effect built up with coloured glazes carefully blended to create a clouding of the surface. If you have the time and patience, you can build this up in several layers with brushes, rags and sponges. The oil-colour veins are put in with a long-haired pencil brush and/or a bird feather. Figure 14.13 is a series of pictures showing the stages in building up the effect. It is important to remember that the veins in marble are not entirely random, there is always a general direction to them.

METHOD FOR GREY/WHITE MARBLE

1. Paint the surface with white eggshell.

2. Make up all your coloured glazes in advance (the reason will be obvious in a moment). For this

exercise, there is a colourless glaze and a grey glaze. You will also need black oil colour thinned to a creamy consistency with white spirit.

3. Paint on a thin coat of the colourless glaze. This will act as a medium for floating other colours.

4. While the glaze is still wet, dab on a small amount of grey glaze with a rag or sponge, then dab intermittently over the surface. The aim is not to cover the surface but to create a clouding effect. The grey blobs will begin to blend into the colourless glaze.

5. Take a very soft-haired paintbrush and gently stroke the glaze in one direction only (diagonally looks good) with no pressure to blend the grey seamlessly into the clear glaze.

6. You can now create white veins with the pencil brush or bird feather. Dip into white spirit and remove the surplus. Hold the bristles (or blade of the feather) almost, but not quite, flat against the glaze and drag, while rolling, it through the glaze. The direction should generally follow that of the clouding, and you can create some branches. The white spirit produces a 'Red Sea' effect in that the glaze splits to reveal the white base.

7. Repeat the exercise with a small amount of the thinned black oil colour shadowing and occasionally criss-crossing the previous lines.

8. Take a sponge and gently dab the veins, both to remove heavy deposits of paint and to smudge them.

9. Finally, take your soft-haired paintbrush and very gently stroke the veins to soften the outline, stroking along the general direction of the veins.

10. Allow to dry for a couple of days and apply at least two coats of clear satin, or matt varnish.

A final point: the glazing part of the work needs to be done quickly, otherwise it starts to stiffen and will resist manipulation. If necessary, break the work down into sections and do each one in turn.

TORTOISESHELL

MATERIALS AND TOOLS

This is a very dramatic finish, ideal for small decorative items such as boxes or small table tops. Two base colours are commonly used: yellow or red. The typical tortoiseshell blotches are made with burnt sienna and burnt umber artists' oil colour. You will also need large artists' oil brushes to apply the blotches and a soft-haired paintbrush to blend the colours. A yellow base coat creates more of a golden brown tortoiseshell, while red leads to a richer colour. Figure 14.14 show the stages in building up the effect.

METHOD

1. Paint an eggshell base colour and allow it to dry.

2. Paint the surface with a thin coat of colourless glaze (this will be used to float the blotches).

3. Apply small dashes of burnt sienna oil colour, thinned to a creamy consistency, leaving plenty of background visible.

4. Repeating the process with burnt umber, place dashes in the spaces between the sienna – but again leave some background visible. The dashes of both colours must be in the same direction.

5. Take a soft-haired paintbrush and gently stroke the dashes along their length to blur and blend into the typical tortoiseshell pattern. Allow to dry before varnishing.

MILK (CASEIN) PAINT

With a book that concerns itself with traditional and modern finishing materials and techniques, the gradual rise in popularity of paints based on traditional organic materials is worthy of inclusion.

One of the problems with the 'industrial' finishes (and that includes modern paints) is that many people are sensitive to the materials used in them. This has led to a slow growth in interest in organic paints. The most common of these is casein paint, traditionally referred

STAGES IN BUILDING UP A TORTOISESHELL EFFECT

Fig 14.14 (a) Yellow eggshell basecoat.

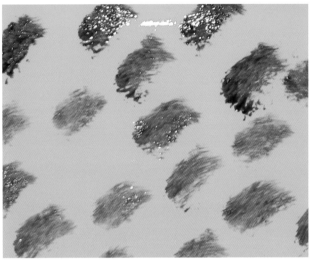

Fig 14.14 (b) Dabs of thinned burnt sienna oil colour.

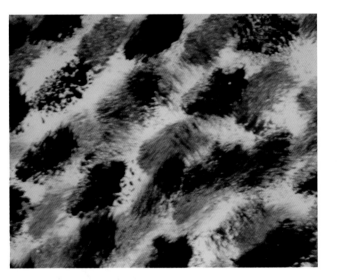

Fig 14.14 (c) Dabs of thinned burnt umber oil colour positioned between burnt sienna patches.

Fig 14.14 (d) The whole surface softened with a brush in one direction to merge the colour into the classic tortoiseshell pattern.

to as 'milk paint', as casein is the main protein component of milk. Also, historically, milk paint was made with the white stuff. This may seem quite odd, because milk is famously perishable, but when milk paint dries it is incredibly durable (although somewhat susceptible to damp conditions).

The basic components of milk paint are skimmed milk, hydrated lime (builders' lime), whiting (to create bulk and opacity) and a suitable colorant. The proportion of whiting to colorant depends on the depth of colour – the more whiting, the paler the

shade, which eventually becomes a pastel. The milk and the lime react together to create calcium caseinate, which binds the whiting and colouring agent as a paint-film when dry.

But, why bother when there are so many good paint products around? The reason is the look it generates. Milk paint creates a soft, matt finish that was typical of old paint, so it can be used to recreate old rustic painted items, and is particularly good for colour-washing effects.

A recipe for milk paint can be found in Chapter 16.

Limed Oak

Lime-wash has a very long pedigree as a decorative finish, dating back to the Middle Ages. It is normally associated with painting internal and external walls of buildings, sometimes coloured with natural plant or mineral pigments to create warmly coloured façades.

If limestone or chalk is baked at a high temperature the result is 'quicklime', which forms the basis of lime-wash. Quicklime reacts vigorously with water, creating 'slaked lime'. When the slaked lime is stirred up with the water in which it was slaked, it forms the basic lime-wash which was painted onto plaster and rendering. The material naturally bonds with the plaster or rendering and hardens to form the decorative finish. While not very durable, it is an easy matter to repaint the walls every year.

When lime-wash was applied to decorative and structural timbers, which in the Middle Ages would have been oak, the decorative effect was rather different. The lime lodged in the open grain, eventually hardening over time, but remained powdery on the surface so it could be wiped or brushed off. This was limed oak. The lime would also have the effect of darkening oak, so there was a sharp contrast which created the decorative effect. Limed oak is still popular, although the methods and materials have been somewhat updated since the time of the Middle Ages.

Figure 15.1, opposite, shows a contemporary use of liming. The house was built in the 1840s in mock-Tudor style, complete with extensive oak panelling throughout the hall and ground floor reception rooms. At some point, the panelling had been treated to a coat or two of very dark varnish, which made the whole place dark

and drab. The antique oak furniture, which was also dark, was lost within the general gloom. The panelling was stripped and then limed using traditional distemper (see page 157) to recreate a traditional dusty, matt finish. This had several effects, which illustrate the decorative qualities of this finish when applied to highly figured oak:

- There is a general lightening up of the space.

- The general contours and figuring of the wood are enhanced, because the profiles of the mouldings and interesting grain patterns are made more obvious.

- Where there are carvings or turned work (see the small carved area above the door), liming accentuates the three-dimensional relief.

- The effect is to create a light and airy backdrop to other features, such as the antique furniture in Fig 15.1 (overleaf).

LIMING VERSUS COLOUR WASHING

Liming does not have to be restricted to use on oak, and any other open-grained timber, such as ash, reacts well to the effect. In fact, 'liming' is a finish found on a wide variety of wooden objects. For example, Fig 15.2, on page 157, shows a section of a pine wall-mirror frame. Its main decorative feature is that the reed moulding and liming has been used to emphasize this, with the 'lime' accumulating in the hollows of the reeded surface. In general, liming really only works in the traditional sense on open-grained surfaces, as the aim is not to create a

Fig 15.1 Limed oak panelling.

heavy surface accumulation, but to highlight grain texture. The effect in Fig 15.2 (opposite) is more like a colour wash, which is exactly what it is, serving to simulate a limed effect (see Chapter 14 for a description of colour washing).

LIMING MATERIALS

Traditional liming is both messy, time-consuming and not entirely without some risk of chemical burns, as slaking quicklime generates a great deal of heat. There is also a preference for a 'blond' effect, which traditional liming does not create. The use of highly alkaline material on oak causes it to darken. There are, however, a number of materials that simulate traditional liming.

LIMING WAX

Liming wax is probably the easiest liming material to use. It is simply a paste made of wax polish and a strong white pigment, such as titanium white. You can either buy liming wax ready-made or, if you prefer, make your own.

While this is an easy way to create a limed effect, it is based on wax and so suffers from the main disadvantage of waxed finishes (see Chapter 6), i.e. it is not durable and hates any handling. Consequently, it is really only suitable for objects and surfaces that are not intended to take any wear. It is ideal for panelling and items such as the mirror frame shown in Fig 15.1. If you intend to lime furniture such as tables or kitchen cabinets, it may be better to use one of the other liming

Fig 15.2 A 'limed', reed-moulded pine mirror frame. The effect is more like colour washing than true liming.

materials listed below, as the finish quickly shows signs of wear, producing dark, grubby patches where the items are habitually handled.

On the other hand, liming wax is a 'renewable' finish, which means that it can be removed or repaired with relative ease, and the ease with which it can be applied makes it a cost-effective finish for large areas. In addition to the 'lime' deposited in the grain, the wax base results in a low lustre over the work.

PAINT

A good alternative to liming wax that is both more durable in its own right and can be over-coated with a hard durable finish such as varnish, French polish, or cellulose lacquer is paint, or pigmented lacquer.

The basic material is thinned oil or water-based paint, and this becomes lodged in the pores of the wood to create the limed effect. The disadvantage of this approach is that you are committed to this as a more or less permanent decorative effect. It is notoriously difficult to get paint out of the grain, even with paint stripper. This does, of course, make it ideal for furniture and objects that will take some wear (e.g. tables, kitchen and bedroom cabinets).

Once protected by a clear, hard finish, it is as durable as you can make it.

The overall look is less traditional than liming wax, or the distemper described below, as the work has an obvious coating of clear varnish or lacquer, but the decorative effect remains the same.

PREPARING THE PAINT

Prepare the paint in a paint kettle and make enough for the whole job, even if it means that you will make too much. Use:

- White oil-based undercoat: this is a heavily pigmented paint designed to give good obliteration of the existing surface colour, and so tends to be quite viscous. Thin with white spirit to the consistency of water. Use white rather than brilliant white undercoat, if you can.

- Matt water-based emulsion: good quality emulsion paint also tends to be quite thick and jelly-like. It needs to be diluted with water until it is runny.

MILK PAINT/DISTEMPER

For a look as closely authentic to traditional liming as you can get, milk paint or distemper is as good as it gets. While not an easy finish to prepare, the result is a soft, dusty, matt finish. The hall in Fig 15.1 would be an obvious candidate for liming wax. This would have created a clean, obvious lustre on the wood, but the client wanted the look of traditional lime. The end result is a limed effect, with a look that is indistinguishable from traditional liming, but which is safer to use.

Chapter 14 describes how to make these paints but, to use them as liming materials, they have to be made rather thinner than for use as a paint. A watery consistency is probably about right, but you may need to experiment on scrap wood to check this. Below I describe how to prepare a surface for liming, and this includes advice about sealing the surface prior to liming, to prevent excessive absorption and a greater contrast. In the case of distemper or milk paint, you may want to omit this to create a more 'dusty' look – but experiment first.

SURFACE PREPARATION

The protocols described in Chapter 4 apply here. The timber to be limed is prepared in exactly the same way as for other finishes. Sometimes, you may need to renew an existing limed finish because of wear, and the method for doing that is described in this section.

NEW OR STRIPPED SURFACES

New surfaces should not present too many problems or challenges, but working with a surface that has been stripped of another finish may need some extra care. The effect of liming requires easy entry of the white deposit into the open grain.

- Sand until smooth in the usual way (see Chapter 4) and remove all dust.

- Open up the grain with a wire brush worked lightly along the grain (see Fig 15.3).

- Lightly sand with 320 grit abrasive to remove any torn fibres and remove dust, especially from the grain. A blast of air from a small compressor is useful for this.

- Liming tends to be seen on light wood, but there is absolutely no reason why the work should not be stained darker first. In fact, the contrast between the dark wood and the white 'lime' produces a more dramatic effect than seen on a blond oak finish (see Fig 15.4).

Fig 15.3 Use a wire brush to open up the grain.

STRIPPED SURFACES

Make sure there is no residue of the old finish, as this will resist the entry of 'lime' into the pores. It may also be necessary to bleach the work after stripping, before preparing it for liming, especially if a dark stain was used originally, which would be obvious in the open grain and make the liming look distinctly odd.

SEALING THE SURFACE

The aim is to create a contrast between the grain and the body of the wood. You can improve this by giving a quick sealing coat of transparent French polish applied by brush. If you are using thinned emulsion paint as the 'liming' agent, this is essential as the pigments are so strong and the binding agents so powerful you run the risk of simply creating a colour-washed effect.

Fig 15.4 (a) Blond limed oak.

It is less of an issue with liming wax, but sealing the work first does make it easier to clear away any residue later and will save on wax.

EXISTING LIMED SURFACES

Renovating an existing limed finish can be a difficult, and is certainly a messy, task. The one problem with liming is that it is not durable if handled too much, which is why it is best applied to surfaces such as wall panelling. On furniture or doors, those areas that are constantly handled eventually become black over time, with most traces of the liming disappearing. That effect is obviously unattractive and disfiguring. If milk paint or distemper has been used, there is a little more durability, but not much. On the other hand, if paint is the liming agent, it is likely to have been protected by a coat or two of varnish or lacquer, making it very durable for such things as kitchen cabinets and occasional tables.

For a complete renovation, you will need to clear out the grain as well as clean the surface, and this is difficult if paint has been used.

Fig 15.4 (b) Stained and limed oak.

LIMING WAX, MILK PAINT AND DISTEMPER

These finishes can be cleaned with warm water and detergent, using a hard scrubbing brush to remove the dirt and to clear the grain. Once the damaged areas of the surface and grain are clear, you need to leave the wood to dry out. Use a wire brush to open up the grain before liming. If you are using a different liming technique, you will need to clean off all the existing liming material.

PAINT

Paint is difficult to remove from the grain, so you need to consider very carefully the alternatives. Can the surface be repaired superficially – i.e. can the protective varnish or lacquer be gently rubbed down and recoated? This is certainly the better option if you can get away with it.

If the surface is so badly damaged and dirty that cleaning off completely is the only realistic option, then opt for tackling only the damaged area. You will need to strip off the protective varnish or lacquer with paint and varnish stripper. The grain will retain the paint 'lime'. Now you can make a decision. If the 'lime' is intact, you might be able to get away with simply revarnishing the area. If not, you will need to clear out the grain and re-lime. This is where it can get difficult.

Fig 15.5 Wiping off excess paint.

Soak the surface with paint stripper for 10–15 minutes before using a fine wire brush to clear out as much paint as you can. You may have to do this several times to completely clear out the grain. Finally, neutralize the residual stripper and allow to dry. then lightly sand to remove raised or torn fibres.

APPLYING THE LIMED FINISH

LIMING WAX

1. Seal the surface with a quick wash of transparent French polish and allow to dry for a couple of hours.

2. Rub a generous amount of liming wax over the surface with a strong, lint-free cloth to force the paste into the grain.

3. Once the surface has been covered, rub lightly across the direction of the grain to remove surplus wax from the surface without lifting it out of the pores.

4. Leave to dry for five to ten minutes before buffing with a soft cloth.

5. For added protection and additional sheen, you can apply a coat of clear wax polish.

MILK PAINT OR DISTEMPER

1. The surface must be sealed whenever paint is used as the liming medium. If you do not, the paint will simply soak into the wood, as well as the open pores, and effectively create a lime-washed effect.

Use transparent French polish as the sealer and leave for a couple of hours to dry.

2. The paint will be quite watery and you need to guard against runs. Apply the paint thinly with a paintbrush, but only cover an area that can be worked within the time the paint remains wet.

3. While it is still wet and fluid, wipe off the surplus with a clean rag, working across the grain so as not to pull the paint out of the grain (see Fig 15.5, on facing page), then wipe lightly along the grain direction with a clean cloth. Clear the surface as much as you can before moving on to the next section of the work.

4. Allow plenty of time for the paint to dry. If the work is a little too cloudy, you can sand it lightly along the grain to clear the surface. Dust off the work.

The beauty of this form of liming is the slightly dusty look it gives to the surface – very similar to the surface of real liming. It should be left unfinished, i.e. no varnish or wax polish, as this would 'kill' the effect.

EMULSION OR UNDERCOAT PAINT

Apply in exactly the same way as milk paint or distemper, including a final sand to clear the surface of residual colour. Finally, you can protect the surface with a coat or two of varnish (matt or satin looks best).

Paint is ideal as a liming agent for furniture that will take a lot of wear, or is in a hostile environment such as a kitchen or bathroom, as it is a durable finish.

16 Recipes for Finishes

SAFETY CONSIDERATIONS

Chapter 3 looks at safety considerations in detail, but a reminder of two of the key hazards, which are:

- **SOLVENTS:** many of the recipes described here require the use of solvents, either cold or warmed, resulting in increased level of vapours in the environment. It is essential to ensure that you have adequate ventilation and advisable to wear a respirator mask.
- **HEAT:** There is a real fire risk with some of the procedures described in this chapter – heating solvents and waxes – so choose a heat source without a naked flame. An electric ring is not entirely without risk, so an electric halogen hob is ideal. In any event, solvents and waxes should not be heated directly, but warmed in a double boiler. This prevents the materials from over-heating (maximum temperature will be 100°C and is usually less). Take precautions against burns and scalds by, for example, wearing protective clothing and eye-protectors.

POLISH REVIVERS

GENERAL PURPOSE REVIVER
1 part (by volume) raw linseed oil
1 part white vinegar
1 part white spirit or pure turpentine
1 part methylated spirits

This is a mixture of water- and oil-soluble materials, which means that they will separate into layers in the bottle. N.B. The bottle should not be plastic, as it might be partially dissolved by the white spirit or turpentine. Keep it emulsified by shaking the bottle well as you use the reviver. This reviver, used sparingly, is very effective on French polished or varnished surfaces that are not too dirty.

HEAVY DUTY REVIVER
1oz (25g) beeswax
1oz (25g) paraffin wax
2oz (50g) soap
1 pint (500ml) white spirit or pure turpentine
1 pint (500ml) water

1. Use soap flakes or shred a bar of soap and dissolve it in hot water. Use a large, old pan for this (the reason will be obvious in step 4). Keep the water and soap mixture simmering on a low heat while you prepare the waxes.
2. Melt the waxes in a double boiler over a low heat, electricity rather than gas, which presents a fire a risk.
3. Once the wax has melted, remove the double boiler from the heat and carefully add the white spirit or turpentine. This will solidify the wax initially, but as the hot water warms up the liquid it will melt again. Return it to the low electric heat to melt and make sure that the waxes are completely melted again.
4. Remove the waxes from the heat and carefully pour them into the hot soapy water. The mixture will begin to emulsify. Remove the mixture from the heat and stir to help it emulsify, otherwise it will separate. You could buy a second-hand freestanding food mixer specifically for this, as you must keep the

mixture agitated until cool if you want to make sure it does not separate.

5. When it is cool, the cream should be stored in an airtight, non-plastic container.

This reviver is a powerful cleaner as well as polish reviver. If a surface is very heavily soiled, you should wash it down with a weak solution of washing soda first.

WAX POLISH

TRADITIONAL BEESWAX POLISH

4oz (100g) white or yellow beeswax
(OR 3$^{1}/_{2}$oz (90g) beeswax and $^{1}/_{2}$oz (10g) carnauba wax)
+ 4fl oz (100ml) pure turpentine or white spirit
N.B. *The alternative mix of carnauba and beeswax produces a slightly harder polish, with a higher sheen.*

1. Melt the wax in a double boiler, over an electric heat to reduce the fire risk.
2. Once the wax has completely melted, carefully and slowly pour in the turpentine or white spirit. The wax will solidify immediately, so maintain the heat and stir until the wax has dissolved completely in the solvent.
3. Remove from the heat and pour the hot liquid into a sealable, non-plastic and wide-necked container. Seal with the lid immediately and store somewhere temporarily, while it cools and solidifies.

ANTIQUE OR DISTRESSING WAX POLISH

The basic recipe and preparation is the same, but the polish is coloured with artists' oil colours. To simulate age and accumulated dirt you should use the earth pigments, such as raw and burnt umber, and lamp black.

Add a small amount of white spirit or pure turpentine to the colour to liquefy it before mixing with, and dispersing throughout, the white spirit or pure turpentine used to make the polish (step 2 in the recipe above).

The amount of colour to use is a matter of judgement and will depend on the degree of distressing and colour-balance required.

BEESWAX CREAM

4oz (100g) of beeswax
1oz (25g) of pure soap
6fl oz (150ml) turpentine or white spirit
6fl oz (150 ml) water

1. Shred the soap and place it in the water. Heat until the soap is dissolved, but do not allow it to boil.
2. Shred the wax into the turpentine or white spirit and heat in a double boiler to dissolve the wax.
3. Remove the wax solution and soapy water from the heat. Quickly pour the wax solution into the soapy water and stir to mix thoroughly. It should turn milky within a few seconds as the mixture emulsifies. You must continue stirring as the mixture cools, otherwise the liquids will separate again. An old food mixer on slow revolutions is ideal for this work.
4. You can add a few drops of lemon essence or any essential oil (such as lavender) to give it a nice smell once it is has started to thicken.
5. Store in an airtight container.

OIL POLISH

(*Ingredients are measured by volume*)
1 part raw linseed oil (or other vegetable oil)
3 parts turpentine or white spirit
1 part terebene (optional)

Mix the ingredients and store in an airtight container. You can add a few drops of essential oil (such as lemon or lavender) to provide a pleasant smell. The terebene is optional, but it is a drying agent and speeds up the hardening of the oil. The turpentine or white spirit

NOTE

Earth pigments work well, but any chemically inert dyeing agent will probably do – you will need to experiment.

If you want a strong colour, omit some or all of the whiting and replace with pure pigment.

dilutes the oil and helps its absorption into the surface of the wood. You can substitute any vegetable oil for linseed if you wish. This oil polish dries quickly, usually overnight.

WAX FILLER STICKS

Either pure beeswax or a 50/50 beeswax/carnauba wax mixture
Artists' oil colour, diluted a little with turpentine or white spirit
Mould, made from metal foil

The beeswax and carnauba wax mixture produces a harder filler than wax on its own. Use oil colours that match the timber to be filled. You will always make more than you need so, over time, you will build up a stock of various colours.

1. Melt the wax in a double boiler (use enough to fill the mould you are using).
2. While the wax is melting, liquefy a quantity of oil colour with a very small amount of turpentine or white spirit, so that it is fluid but not 'watery'.
3. Once all the wax has melted, pour in the colour and stir to mix. Make sure there is enough colour to make the waxes opaque and have a 'solid' colour.
4. When thoroughly mixed, carefully pour the wax into the mould and set aside to cool and solidify. The mould can be peeled away from the solid block once it is cool.

TRADITIONAL MILK PAINT

(*Quantities given by volume or weight*)
10 parts skimmed milk
1 part hydrated lime (builders' lime)
8 parts whiting (from artists' suppliers)
Pure pigments to colour

1. Add the hydrated lime to the milk and mix thoroughly to make a smooth liquid.
2. Add the whiting to the mixture, to create a basic opaque white paint, and mix to a smooth consistency.

3. Mix in the pigment to reach the desired colour, i.e. a pastel version of the pigment colour.

The paint must be used the same day, or certainly within two days, refrigerating overnight. The lime and the milk are critical to the success of this paint: the casein in the milk reacts with the calcium in the lime to produce calcium caseinate, a natural binding agent.

TRANSPARENT GLAZES AND WASHES

Glazes and washes are vulnerable even after drying, because they form a very thin coat. Protect the surface with a clear varnish.

OIL GLAZE
1 part raw linseed oil
1 part white spirit or pure turpentine
1 teaspoon (5ml) terebene per 1pt (500ml) glaze
Artists' oil colour

This produces a very liquid glaze, so apply it thinly to prevent runs. Colour with artists' oil colour, which has first been thinned with white spirit or turpentine, to make it liquid. The glaze is very transparent, unless strongly coloured.

The terebene accelerates the drying time of this glaze, but it still takes a couple of days to reach maximum hardness. It should be left to fully harden before varnishing, otherwise you risk displacing the glaze.

WATER-BASED GLAZE (WASH)
1 part wallpaper paste (mixed to normal consistency with water)
Artists' acrylic or watercolour

Wallpaper paste gives the colour a 'stiffness' on the work which allows it to be easily manipulated, and retards the drying time of the artists' colour. Liquefy the colour with a little water before mixing with the paste.

This glaze will dry within a few of hours in a warm environment. It remains workable for a shorter period than oil-based glaze, so you need to work quickly.

About the Author

I an Hosker has practised as a furniture restorer and French polisher for more than a quarter of a century, and has taught the subject in further and community education establishments since 1981. His books are the product of those years of practising and teaching his craft. He first gained his skills from his grandfather when, as a teenager, natural curiosity led him to want to learn the craft.

What began as natural adolescent curiosity grew into a passion for furniture and its restoration, which resulted in Ian setting up in business as an antique furniture restorer and French polisher.

In 1989 Ian moved from NW England to Devon, England, where he has continued to teach and write on the subject. At the time of writing this book he has taught an estimated 1000–1500 students various aspects of the craft.

Index

TITLES AVAILABLE FROM
GMC Publications

BOOKS

WOODCARVING

Beginning Woodcarving	GMC Publications
Carving Architectural Detail in Wood: The Classical Tradition	Frederick Wilbur
Carving Birds & Beasts	GMC Publications
Carving Classical Styles in Wood	Frederick Wilbur
Carving the Human Figure: Studies in Wood and Stone	Dick Onians
Carving Nature: Wildlife Studies in Wood	Frank Fox-Wilson
Celtic Carved Lovespoons: 30 Patterns	Sharon Littley & Clive Griffin
Decorative Woodcarving (New Edition)	Jeremy Williams
Elements of Woodcarving	Chris Pye
Figure Carving in Wood: Human and Animal Forms	Sara Wilkinson
Lettercarving in Wood: A Practical Course	Chris Pye
Relief Carving in Wood: A Practical Introduction	Chris Pye
Woodcarving for Beginners	GMC Publications
Woodcarving Made Easy	Cynthia Rogers
Woodcarving Tools, Materials & Equipment (New Edition in 2 vols.)	Chris Pye

WOODTURNING

Bowl Turning Techniques Masterclass	Tony Boase
Chris Child's Projects for Woodturners	Chris Child
Decorating Turned Wood: The Maker's Eye	Liz & Michael O'Donnell
Green Woodwork	Mike Abbott
A Guide to Work-Holding on the Lathe	Fred Holder
Keith Rowley's Woodturning Projects	Keith Rowley
Making Screw Threads in Wood	Fred Holder
Segmented Turning: A Complete Guide	Ron Hampton
Turned Boxes: 50 Designs	Chris Stott
Turning Green Wood	Michael O'Donnell
Turning Pens and Pencils	Kip Christensen & Rex Burningham
Wood for Woodturners	Mark Baker
Woodturning: Forms and Materials	John Hunnex
Woodturning: A Foundation Course (New Edition)	Keith Rowley
Woodturning: A Fresh Approach	Robert Chapman
Woodturning: An Individual Approach	Dave Regester
Woodturning: A Source Book of Shapes	John Hunnex
Woodturning Masterclass	Tony Boase
Woodturning Projects: A Workshop Guide to Shapes	Mark Baker

WOODWORKING

Beginning Picture Marquetry	Lawrence Threadgold
Carcass Furniture	GMC Publications
Celtic Carved Lovespoons: 30 Patterns	Sharon Littley & Clive Griffin
Celtic Woodcraft	Glenda Bennett
Celtic Woodworking Projects	Glenda Bennett
Complete Woodfinishing (Revised Edition)	Ian Hosker
David Charlesworth's Furniture-Making Techniques	David Charlesworth
David Charlesworth's Furniture-Making Techniques – Volume 2	David Charlesworth
Furniture Projects with the Router	Kevin Ley
Furniture Restoration (Practical Crafts)	Kevin Jan Bonner
Furniture Restoration: A Professional at Work	John Lloyd
Furniture Workshop	Kevin Ley
Green Woodwork	Mike Abbott
History of Furniture: Ancient to 1900	Michael Huntley
Intarsia: 30 Patterns for the Scrollsaw	John Everett
Making Heirloom Boxes	Peter Lloyd
Making Screw Threads in Wood	Fred Holder
Making Woodwork Aids and Devices	Robert Wearing
Mastering the Router	Ron Fox
Pine Furniture Projects for the Home	Dave Mackenzie
Router Magic: Jigs, Fixtures and Tricks to Unleash your Router's Full Potential	Bill Hylton
Router Projects for the Home	GMC Publications
Router Tips & Techniques	Robert Wearing
Routing: A Workshop Handbook	Anthony Bailey
Routing for Beginners (Revised and Expanded Edition)	Anthony Bailey
Stickmaking: A Complete Course	Andrew Jones & Clive George
Stickmaking Handbook	Andrew Jones & Clive George
Storage Projects for the Router	GMC Publications
Success with Sharpening	Ralph Laughton
Veneering: A Complete Course	Ian Hosker
Veneering Handbook	Ian Hosker
Wood: Identification & Use	Terry Porter
Woodworking Techniques and Projects	Anthony Bailey
Woodworking with the Router: Professional Router Techniques any Woodworker can Use	Bill Hylton & Fred Matlack

UPHOLSTERY

Upholstery: A Beginners' Guide	David James
Upholstery: A Complete Course (Revised Edition)	David James
Upholstery Restoration	David James
Upholstery Techniques & Projects	David James
Upholstery Tips and Hints	David James

DOLLS' HOUSES AND MINIATURES

$^1/_{12}$ Scale Character Figures for the Dolls' House	James Carrington
Americana in $^1/_{12}$ Scale: 50 Authentic Projects	Joanne Ogreenc & Mary Lou Santovec
The Authentic Georgian Dolls' House	Brian Long
A Beginners' Guide to the Dolls' House Hobby	Jean Nisbett
Celtic, Medieval and Tudor Wall Hangings in $^1/_{12}$ Scale Needlepoint	Sandra Whitehead
Creating Decorative Fabrics: Projects in $^1/_{12}$ Scale	Janet Storey
Dolls' House Accessories, Fixtures and Fittings	Andrea Barham
Dolls' House Furniture: Easy-to-Make Projects in $^1/_{12}$ Scale	Freida Gray
Dolls' House Makeovers	Jean Nisbett

CRAFTS

Three-Dimensional Découpage:
    Innovative Projects for Beginners   *Hilda Stokes*
Trompe l'Oeil: Techniques and Projects   *Jan Lee Johnson*
Tudor Treasures to Embroider   *Pamela Warner*
Wax Art   *Hazel Marsh*

PHOTOGRAPHY

Close-Up on Insects   *Robert Thompson*
Digital Enhancement
    for Landscape Photographers   *Arjan Hoogendam & Herb Parkin*
Double Vision   *Chris Weston & Nigel Hicks*
An Essential Guide to Bird Photography   *Steve Young*
Field Guide to Bird Photography   *Steve Young*
Field Guide to Landscape Photography   *Peter Watson*
How to Photograph Pets   *Nick Ridley*
In my Mind's Eye: Seeing in Black and White   *Charlie Waite*
Life in the Wild: A Photographer's Year   *Andy Rouse*
Light in the Landscape: A Photographer's Year *Peter Watson*
Photographers on Location with Charlie Waite   *Charlie Waite*
Photographing Wilderness   *Jason Friend*
Photographing your Garden   *Gail Harland*
Photography for the Naturalist   *Mark Lucock*
Photojournalism: An Essential Guide   *David Herrod*
Professional Landscape and Environmental Photography:
    From 35mm to Large Format   *Mark Lucock*
Rangefinder   *Roger Hicks & Frances Schultz*
Underwater Photography   *Paul Kay*
Where and How to Photograph Wildlife   *Peter Evans*
Wildlife Photography Workshops   *Steve & Ann Toon*

ART TECHNIQUES

Beginning Watercolours   *Bee Morrison*
Oil Paintings from the Landscape:
    A Guide for Beginners   *Rachel Shirley*
Oil Paintings from your Garden: A Guide for Beginners *Rachel Shirley*
Sketching Landscapes in Pen and Pencil   *Joyce Percival*

VIDEOS

Drop-in and Pinstuffed Seats   *David James*
Stuffover Upholstery   *David James*
Elliptical Turning   *David Springett*
Woodturning Wizardry   *David Springett*
Turning Between Centres: The Basics   *Dennis White*
Turning Bowls   *Dennis White*
Boxes, Goblets and Screw Threads   *Dennis White*
Novelties and Projects   *Dennis White*
Classic Profiles   *Dennis White*
Twists and Advanced Turning   *Dennis White*
Sharpening the Professional Way   *Jim Kingshott*
Sharpening Turning & Carving Tools   *Jim Kingshott*
Bowl Turning   *John Jordan*
Hollow Turning   *John Jordan*
Woodturning: A Foundation Course   *Keith Rowley*
Carving a Figure: The Female Form   *Ray Gonzalez*
The Router: A Beginner's Guide   *Alan Goodsell*
The Scroll Saw: A Beginner's Guide   *John Burke*

MAGAZINES

WOODTURNING
WOODCARVING
FURNITURE & CABINETMAKING
THE ROUTER
NEW WOODWORKING
THE DOLLS' HOUSE MAGAZINE
OUTDOOR PHOTOGRAPHY
BLACK & WHITE PHOTOGRAPHY
KNITTING
GUILD NEWS

The above represents a full list of all titles currently published or scheduled to be published.
All are available direct from the Publishers or through bookshops, newsagents and specialist retailers.
To place an order, or to obtain a complete catalogue, contact:

GMC Publications,
Castle Place, 166 High Street, Lewes, East Sussex BN7 1XU United Kingdom
Tel: 01273 488005 Fax: 01273 402866
E-mail: pubs@thegmcgroup.com
Website: www.gmcbooks.com

Orders by credit card are accepted